The Algorithmic Anarchist

Table of Contents

The Algorithmic Anarchist..7
    Put Your Notes Here:..10
    Absolutes..11
    Affichage Libre...12
    Alternative Currency...13
    Android..14
    API...14
    Apps...15
    Artificial Intelligence...16
    Artwashing...17
    Bail In..18
    Big Data...19
    Blinding...20
    Bollards...21
    Bots..22
    Boycott..22
    Brands...23
    Brandalism..25
    Bullshit Gesture, The...25
    Cash...26
    Cashless Society..27
    Citizen Science..28
    Cloward–Piven..29
    Clutter...30
    Co-Creation...31
    Colonise..32

Competition..33
Consciousness-Raising................................34
Consultations..35
Cooperation...35
Crash on Demand.....................................36
Credit...36
Credit Cards..37
Cryptocurrency...37
Delete Me..38
Demonstrations..38
Depave...39
Echo Chamber..40
Encryption..41
Energy...42
Engagement..44
Facebook...45
Fair Value..45
FAQ...47
Free Software..49
Friction..49
Gardening...50
Generosity...52
GPS..53
Grant Funding..53
Guerilla Gardening...................................55
Hackathon...56
Hierarchy of Evil......................................57
Hieroglyphics..58
Hipsters...58
Import Substitution..................................59
Industry...60
Interstitial..61

Kulaks	62
Linux	63
Loyalty Cards	65
Machine Intelligence	65
Mercenaries	65
Meta	66
Mischief	67
Models	68
Mitigation	69
Money	70
Music	72
Narrative	73
Open Everything	75
Open Source	76
Parallel Structures	77
People's AI	78
Port-80	78
Port-443	79
Printed Supplements	80
Public Key Cryptography	80
Récuperation	81
Scarcity	82
Search-engine	83
Security Tools	84
Smart Meters	85
Spectacle	87
Speed	88
Sponsorship	89
Street Art	90
Subsidiarity	92
System, The	93
They	94

Think Tanks...95
Trolling..95
Vectorialist...96
Via Negativa..97
Volunteering..98
Walled Gardens...99
What is to be Done?..100
WMD...101
Written Record..101
Unconference..102
Utopia..104
Two Essays..106
  Sense and Sensor Networks..106
    Introduction..106
    Sense and Measure...108
    Social Policy via Rewards..109
    Invent and Communicate...111
    And That's It..112
  A Green Micro-Economy..113
    Introduction..113
    The Economy Itself..115
  Cover It All With Green..119
Library 451:..123
  Fit the First: Looking for 'books'..123
  Fit the Second: Interrogating the 'library'..................................125
  Fit the Third: Where We Are Now..129
The Municipal Green Opportunity...130
  Introduction..130
  Argument..135
  Solutions..139
    The Material..148
    The Technical...150

The Social..152
Conclusions..158
Bibliography...162

The Algorithmic Anarchist   Hugh Barnard 24/10/21

Put Your Notes Here:

The Algorithmic Anarchist

I'm both a philosophical anarchist[1], a computer scientist, and a child of the 1960s. So, without sitting in the British Library and growing a bushy beard, I've decided to write something observational, commentary on the status quo, resistance, and micro-projects. I hope it's non-technical, opinionated (it is), and playful rather than ponderous.

I've organised the principal text alphabetically by subject with a little cross-referencing. There are footnotes in the print version which are hyperlinks in the electronic version which is freely available on my website at https://hughbarnard.org[2]. There are lots of footnotes because I'd like this to be a source book as well, especially as libraries are being neutered as described in the last essay **Library 451**.

For random explanations, start with Wikipedia[3] or better, for philosophy, the Stanford Encyclopedia of Philosophy[4]. We live in a wonderful time for open learning.

---

1 https://en.wikipedia.org/wiki/Philosophical_anarchism
2 http://hughbarnard.org/
3 https://en.wikipedia.org/wiki/Main_Page
4 https://plato.stanford.edu/

The Algorithmic Anarchist   Hugh Barnard 24/10/21

The level of the principal text is (I hope) non-academic. The essays at the end are probably a little more challenging. Wikipedia is pretty good for scientific, mathematical and 'factual' information, if sketchy, but can be bad for disputed topics, because of aggressive editing, see, for example, the the Philip Cross[5] mystery and controversy.

People may (rightly) feel that these shorter texts are a little choppy. However, they relieve me from the burden of inventing some over-arching ideological theme to unify the whole work. Anyway, *I fear frameworks, right, left, and centre*. I believe Utopianism is a tool and a thought experiment, not a fixed, 'thing'.

There are prescriptive Utopias (the original[6], for example), descriptive and narrative Utopias (News from Nowhere[7] and a great deal of science fiction) and negotiated utopias, via utopian thinking and discussion. We want different things. However, we all need, at least shelter, warmth, company, and food in adequate amounts. Above that, there is curious but comforting commonality in our taste for the sky, green space and (undefinable but agreed on) natural beauty. I'm not going to start into culture, because I believe Bourdieu[8] who shows that (currently) taste is a function of social class.

---

5   https://wikipedia.fivefilters.org/
6   https://en.wikipedia.org/wiki/Utopia_(book) (incidentally this may be satire!)
7   https://en.wikipedia.org/wiki/News_from_Nowhere
8   https://en.wikipedia.org/wiki/Pierre_Bourdieu

The Algorithmic Anarchist   Hugh Barnard 24/10/21

Also, future statements such as 'there will be a sea battle tomorrow'[9] do not have any truth in them, in general, things do not turn out as you expect. So this is a toolkit with connecting subjects rather than any grand unifying theory. I'm bound to be wrong about some things, it's the human condition. Finally, on this subject, the only 'business' book that I like, Up the Organisation[10], is organised like this, so I am happy to borrow the organisation and give attribution to the idea.

In terms of influence, here are some in no particular order, The Whole Earth Catalog[11], Alternative London[12], Undercurrents[13] (I was there for a short while), the Global Ideas Bank[14] (also there), the Situationists[15] and their antecedents, the Merry Pranksters[16] and Yippies[17], Tom Wolfe and the humour of Bill Hicks. There are probably many others that will appear in the detail, I do not believe that there are very many truly original bits of thought, and they are probably not in here. I am an integration engineer not an originator.

OK, so let's begin. Lots of space for your notes too. If you want to comment or add for the next editing cycle, write to hugh.barnard@hughbarnard.org. Share and enjoy!

---

9   https://plato.stanford.edu/entries/future-contingents/
10 https://www.goodreads.com/en/book/show/546936.Up_the_Organization
11 https://en.wikipedia.org/wiki/Whole_Earth_Catalog
12 https://en.wikipedia.org/wiki/Nicholas_Saunders_(activist)
13 https://en.wikipedia.org/wiki/Undercurrents_(magazine)
14 https://en.wikipedia.org/wiki/Global_Ideas_Bank
15 https://en.wikipedia.org/wiki/Situationist_International
16 https://en.wikipedia.org/wiki/Merry_Pranksters
17 https://en.wikipedia.org/wiki/Youth_International_Party

The Algorithmic Anarchist   Hugh Barnard 24/10/21

Put Your Notes Here:

The Algorithmic Anarchist   Hugh Barnard 24/10/21

Absolutes

Radicals of all colours tend to get hung up on absolutes. For example 'if we can't boycott X at 100%, forget it'. But actually the world is much more ill-defined and partial, so absolute thinking can be an enemy and, more importantly, a source of perceived powerlessness.

Everyone knows the (incorrect, the frog will jump out) story about frog boiling now, raising the temperature little by little, so that the frog does not notice. Consider the current arrangement of society as the frog and radical change as the water that is heating up as a metaphor for progressive change. Also confrontational change or change involving large discontinuities will almost certainly provoke a) awareness of the process by the status quo b) violent reaction.

This is why I believe, for example, that each home grown carrot, raspberry and salad leaf that is therefore not bought from Tesco, is a small victory. Incidentally, Bristol tried to ban blackberry picking[18] and a council near me cut down several big stands of blackberries for 'security reasons', so the status quo does see alternative sources of food as either disruptive or frankly, a threat. Go, Winstanley[19].

Lastly, on this subject, I agree that things can be too slow, also. However, this is the power of networking too, one carrot at a time for 100K people is 100K carrots out of their system and into 'our' system (however that evolves).

---

18 https://www.bristol247.com/news-and-features/news/council-backs-down-on-blackberry-picking/
19 https://en.wikipedia.org/wiki/Gerrard_Winstanley

The Algorithmic Anarchist   Hugh Barnard 24/10/21

Affichage Libre

I've chosen the French phrase for this[20], because the 'idea' and supporting law doesn't exist in the UK. It ought to. Simply, it's space where any non-profit organisation can advertise. To quote 'douze mètres carrés plus cinq mètres carrés par tranche de 10 000 habitants' and translate 'twelve square metres for each slice of 10k inhabitants' as the space that is *made available by law*.

There are about 350K people in my borough, which would translate to 420 square meters of 'social' publicity. In fact, the libraries do this in a way, but, of course they gatekeep for the powers-that-be so that only approved (normally borough developed and sponsored activities) activities and organisations are included.

It would be interesting to broaden this out and, in fact, it's a social use for electronic billboards, perhaps with a search function on a robust keyboard at the bottom of the installation.
Most councils and municipal organisations in the UK are afraid of this kind of free speech, as it implies a loss of 'their' control. It's always interesting to spend a little time in Cambridge town centre and see how many informal announcements (often on church railings) there are and see that the 'system', when there's a reasonably educated population is self-regulating.

---

20 https://fr.wikipedia.org/wiki/Affichage_libre

The Algorithmic Anarchist   Hugh Barnard 24/10/21

Alternative Currency

This requires a whole book[21], actually. We can divide the subject into alternative and complementary, which are as their names suggest. Mostly, at the moment, we see complementary currencies, currencies that exist alongside a national currency, the Bristol Pound[22] for example. Most of these are, at least, partially convertible into the national currency and therefore are not totally distinct from it. Some of them are grant or government supported too, so they are designed for partial dependence on the current system, not independent from it.

They tend to appear or reappear when the conventional economy is in trouble, there were hundreds of scrip issuances during the US 1930s depression, for example. More recently the truque clubs[23] (in Spanish) in Argentine appeared during the financial crisis in the early 2000s. There's a conspiracy theory that these clubs were undermined by the 'reappearing' central government when they became too widespread and too successful. I wasn't there, so I don't know the truth of that, but it is a clear danger.

There's a lot of scope for experiment and innovation here now, too. For example, cryptocurrencies[24] that have some human governance built into them. In general, I'm not a huge fan of crypto, there's a separate entry for this. It feels like an energy squandering distraction and a clunky technology, but I'm keeping an open mind.

---

21 https://neweconomics.org/2015/05/people-powered-money
22 https://bristolpound.org/
23 http://taoaproject.org/index.php/2010/11/26/historias-de-los-clubes-de-trueque-en-argentina/
24 https://en.wikipedia.org/wiki/Cryptocurrency

Android

I'll just re-quote something I wrote, to wit: "As far as I'm concerned Android[25] is a sticky layer of ugliness, spyiness, syrupiness and general insecurity attached with sticky tape onto the top of a Linux kernel. Most of this shit is written in Java, the COBOL of the 1990s with it's murky license and endless lines of code, to do one little thing."

At least, if you must use it, read one of the articles on securing the phone, this is discussed in more detail in the technical section. I currently feel that the best kind of mobile phone is a feature phone[26], no GPS just phone calls and SMS. I'm not going give any commentary about Apple and iOS (which is also based on another related open source operating system).

API

Short for Application Program Interface. A way of using a piece of software from another piece without touching the internals of the target software. For example, of integrating maps or other data (train times, let's say) into a web site.

Open APIs are not Open Source or Free Software. Open APIs do not necessarily mean Open Data either. Like **Volunteering**, **Hackathon** there is a great deal of bad-faith misrepresentation. One sees corporations saying they are 'open' since they have 'open APIs'. Only when the source code[27] of the software core is downloadable and modifiable do we have anything near open.

---
25 https://en.wikipedia.org/wiki/Android_(operating_system)
26 https://en.wikipedia.org/wiki/Feature_phone
27 https://en.wikipedia.org/wiki/Source_code

The Algorithmic Anarchist   Hugh Barnard 24/10/21

Apps

No, no. Most commercial and (national/local) government apps will take data from you by either stealth or as a result of bad design and/or security measures. I'm not a believer in 'smart' phones either. If you must and want to spend every single moment of your day on Twitter or Facebook, then you'll have a lot less time for the revolution too.

Here are a few random permission strings, from the Android developers website:
READ_CONTACTS WRITE_CONTACTS GET_ACCOUNTS , LOCATION,ACCESS_FINE_LOCATION ACCESS_COARSE_LOCATION, MICROPHONE,RECORD_AUDIO

See what I mean? Incidentally this is often not done with intent, but the results of stupidity without malice can be the same. One of the results of LOCATION for example, is that the App and therefore the originators understand where you are.

Currently, Apps are also a source of externalisation and micro-privatisaton. For example, bus shelters used to have bus arrival displays, these are gradually being abandoned, so the potential passenger will be either 'encourage' to have a phone and App or just wait in a state of unknowing.

Next PSD2, strong authentication[28] in Europe is being used to push customers towards banking Apps (a fruitful source of valuable data) using strong authentication as an excuse. Thus, the sheep are being herded, little by little, towards smart phones.

---

28 https://en.wikipedia.org/wiki/Strong_customer_authentication

The Algorithmic Anarchist   Hugh Barnard 24/10/21

Artificial Intelligence

Most Artificial intelligence "isn't". There are two branches, symbolic AI[29] more popular in the 1980s in the form of expert systems and non-symbolic, statistical and neural networks. It's fair to say that they can be combined to make hybrids too.

The current problem and immediate danger is so-called AI is now used for evaluating credit scores, insurance premiums and other figures that will affect quality of everyone's life. Most of these approaches optimise and do high order correlation[30], rather than do anything particularly intelligent, in the case of corporations, optimise profit, possibly at the expense of exclusion and bias (the lower paid and particular ethnic groups, for example). The output is numeric and they are not (unless some kind of hybrid) explanatory. Also, there may often be non-transparent implicit bias in the input data. These are the proponents of the 'computer says no'[31] activities. There's an additional concern in that human operators are willingly surrendering decisions to these systems, since, for example 'computer says no' is less of a bitter pill and potentially less confrontational than 'I say no'. Happily there's some progress here[32].

Quite a lot of the simpler AI is well understood now and there are many, many open source tools and libraries for producing our own systems, I have written about this in the entry **People's AI**.

---

29 https://en.wikipedia.org/wiki/Symbolic_artificial_intelligence
30 https://en.wikipedia.org/wiki/Correlation
31 https://www.youtube.com/watch?v=AJQ3TM-p2QI
32 https://scitechdaily.com/a-new-nobel-computer-scientist-wins-1-million-artificial-intelligence-prize/

The Algorithmic Anarchist   Hugh Barnard 24/10/21

Artwashing

This is a good introductory article[33] but, basically, putting lipstick on a pig in order to gentrify and *attract investment*. Nice motivational murals where there are many, diverse happy faces (modern) or nostalgia for a past that never existed in the form portrayed by the mural. Artists, who often have to scrape by, are caught in the middle of this, because these represent decent commissions, however they should either a) resist the temptation b) introduce symbolic (say) elements of subversion into the finished mural, as, for example, images animals with symbolic meaning (foxes, hares). Most councils are culturally poor anyway, they probably won't notice.

I'm not against 'street art' but it needs a mandate from the bottom, rather than being pushed down from the top. Currently, as I write, this is going on where I live, a great deal of cash spent, and we are 'voting' for the ones we like best, in my case, none.

There's a huge difference between artwashing and people's art, artefacts of local production and ownership, this might include graffiti, for example. From a middle class perspective it may look like scribbling and scrawling but it is saying something, even if merely 'I exist and was here' and (unhappily) 'this is the territory of our gang'.

---

33 http://colouringinculture.org/blog/artwashingsocialcapitalantigentrification

Bail In

Another reason for physical cash and community backed cash. A bail in is when a failing bank decides to help itself[34] to some (or all, but that hasn't happened so far) of its depositors cash. This may be in return for shares, which are usually nearly worthless, so this is a piece of institutional robbery supported by governments and legitimised by the EU. This happened in Cyprus in 2013[35].

The usual 'canary' for this kind of activity, a form of institutional theft, is legislation that would allow it. As far as I know (I'm not a lawyer or a statue law expert) this kind of legislation exists as least in Canada, Cyprus, New Zealand, the US, the UK, and Germany, as of 2013. There may be more now, so it's an area that would repay further research. Then, just before the act, there's usually narrative or spin about how most of this is dirty money, anyway. That seemed to be the case in Cyprus.

This is also an additional (and strong) argument for more radical (as opposed to state supported, grant funded, half measures) alternative currency systems and people-controlled trading mechanisms.

---

34 https://www.investopedia.com/terms/b/bailin.asp
35 https://www.reuters.com/article/us-cyprus-banks-idUSKBN1K3242

The Algorithmic Anarchist   Hugh Barnard 24/10/21

Big Data

In the case of personal data, the accumulation of enormous quantities of data from loyalty cards, credit cards, debit cards, on-line activity, mobile phone use, credit scores, GPS traces from sports watches, electoral registers and anything else that defines an individual or family.

Before, computers and their storage couldn't handle this quantity of data or process it, now they can, to the detriment of privacy.

There are two additional points here. First, the data can be linked together, for example record A has the same telephone number (say) as record B, then 'we' can produce record C with the accumulated data. Second, this unpleasant accumulation can then be used for **Micro targeting** (see the entry), because someone, often Facebook, knows your age, your voting preferences, your income, your car model and (pace Vonnegut[36]) on and on.

There are many other kinds, from pollution sensors, weather stations and other automated sources. Incidentally there's overlap between this and personal data in, for example, the data provided by smart meters and domestic security systems. Simple example, smart meter data can potentially provide or confirm information about whether a dwelling is occupied and whether someone is using unusual quantities of electricity, which might suggest a pot farm.

---

36 https://en.wikipedia.org/wiki/Kurt_Vonnegut (yes, read him!)

The Algorithmic Anarchist   Hugh Barnard 24/10/21

Blinding

Not as violent as it might sound. The purpose of this is to deny, deprive and remove all (or more realistically, as much as possible) your personal data from **The System**[37], whether you believe this is the Capitalism System, Neo-Liberalism, Big Data or 'whatever'. This is the reason to cut down or abandon credit cards, loyalty cards, promotional emails, turn off GPS, use simple feature phones and not smartphones (they aren't smart, they just provide a method to follow you around, sell you stuff and divide your attention) and any other measure you may think of. Use cash, whenever possible too, debit cards are as bad as credit cards, for tracking you.

Incidentally, since the first draft, it has now been revealed that Google tracked Android users even when the location services were switched off[38] on the phone, so *trust* is not the most realistic default setting for this part of your life.

I found the local police wandering around in the library at time of writing. They wanted people's email addresses, so that they could have *conversations*, do not give email addresses to anyone except your actual correspondents.

I'm still using gmail at the moment but I'm shifting to one of the Swiss based paid providers little by little. That's the downside, you may have to pay for extra privacy.

---

37 I've defined this later, but the current neo-liberal phase of capitalism.
38 https://www.newscientist.com/article/2176663-google-tracks-your-location-even-if-you-switch-off-location-tracking/

The Algorithmic Anarchist   Hugh Barnard 24/10/21

I'm doing this now, it's a pain:
1. Paid the provider and set up the new email
2. Imported all the contacts into my new email
3. Switched on forwarding from the old email to the new
4. Wrote to all my frequent correspondents noting the change
5. Changed at the bank, the council etc.
6. Put a note at the bottom of my old email and new noting the change
7. Clear up exceptions, newsletters etc. piece by piece

I'm thinking of keeping the old gmail open and filled with junk. This is on the same principle of putting surrealist and stilted Marxist requests in Siri, Alex and other assorted cybernetic home-invasion abominations.

Bollards

You didn't expect this entry did you? I had a discussion, more a full and frank exchange of views with a local councillor about bollards. There are two choices here. First we can continuously prevent people doing *bad things* by filling the whole of the public realm with bollards, razor wire, cutting down bushes and trees (so people can't hide weapons, apparently), and removing benches (so kids can't congregate and the homeless can't sleep on them).

Or, second, we can address some of these thing at their roots, persuade people of the virtues[39] of behaving in a different way, in which case we don't need these physical barriers and rearrangements.

There's also an entry on **Clutter**, as in public realm clutter. Needless to say, I am not an enthusiast.

---
39 https://plato.stanford.edu/entries/ethics-virtue/

The Algorithmic Anarchist   Hugh Barnard 24/10/21

Bots

Another subject close to modern AI, but with old, old roots, stretching back to Eliza[40], a program that can try to talk to you and perhaps make you believe, for a while, that it is a person. Lots of uses ranging from the commercial and customer help to sowing some kind of political dissension. Lots of discussion recently about whether bots have contributed to election results, no clear answer.

As the radicals do not seem to have many (or any) bots at the moment and that is a shame, because there is certainly some liberatory mischief to be had, see, for example the **Brandalism** entry. I have been thinking also of some of the ideas in Robert Sheckley's[41] stories and novels, especially the idea of hyper-specialised predator. These do not limit themselves to one species but sometimes down to one individual. Imagine, for example, a little mocking bot that stalks sowing ridicule on the ridiculous.

Boycott

One of the best tools, left in the toolbox. The modern world is run by 'just-in-time'[42] (computer driven ordering) too, so *surgical boycotts* will have immediate and amusing effects. I'm thinking, for example, of one particular size of one particular thing, for a week.

The boycott of the Sun newspaper isn't working too badly either. Even partial electronic boycott, such as *diminishing* orders to Amazon and *substituting* Hive[43] as much as possible, is good.

---

40   https://en.wikipedia.org/wiki/ELIZA
41   https://en.wikipedia.org/wiki/Robert_Sheckley
42   https://en.wikipedia.org/wiki/Lean_manufacturing
43   https://www.hive.co.uk/

The Algorithmic Anarchist   Hugh Barnard 24/10/21

Do not be lured into the trap of believing that if it's not done at 100%, it's not worth it, as preached by the sanctimonious. That way lies paralysis and powerlessness.

One theoretical example, LinkedIn, bought by Microsoft for $26 billion. If everyone left, it's worth zero, no riots, no sit-downs, no police. Because there is network maths involved, even a 10 -15% haemorrhage would hammer it too. Where 'you are the product', you are, in fact, also the 'decider' if you mass together in sufficient numbers. Incidentally, I left LinkedIn the very day Microsoft bought it, actually it's been near useless professionally anyway or, perhaps, I just don't care enough about 'work'. See the entry for Facebook also.

Brands

Oh, they are so sneaky. That Cadbury's fruit and nut, that I used to like is owned by Kraft's which is now absorbed into a global conglomerate called Mondelez. The chocolate making itself has been yanked out of the UK into somewhere in Eastern Europe. Kraft also broke a takeover promise when that happened. So, Mondelez/Cadbury is a prime boycott candidate, until they wither away or change their ways.

However, one can argue, rightly, chocolate is de minimis, one does not live by chocolate alone. So, consider this. The original name for the Sellafield was Windscale[44] and, as such, suffered a fire and release of radioactivity in the late 1950s. But now the installation has become 'Sellafield' and the original problem has been buried in history somewhat. There are problems associated with Sellafield too, perhaps it's time for another name change?

---
44   https://en.wikipedia.org/wiki/Sellafield#Windscale_fire

Another example, Accenture was previously part of Arthur Anderson. As such they were the auditors of the Enron and surrendered their licence as a result of this. The consulting part was split off and became 'Accenture'. Much better. Not.

Finally, Rachel's Organic[45] yoghurt with its cutsie-pie message is part of Lactalis Nestlé (see below), an enormous (61K employees) conglomerate. This is becoming more and more frequent now and is part of what Debord called **Récuperation** which has its own entry here.

So there are several points to take away here, changes of name, changes of ownership (especially concentrations of ownership) and récuperation. There are no databases or tools, as far as I know (and someone please correct me for the next edition) that track all the brands presented by any given conglomerate and stay up to date. For example, the repulsive Nestlé (I am looking at the actual behaviour, the wells etc. rather than the confusing videos, same for Coca-Cola[46]) owns a huge number of brands[47]. In order to effectively boycott Nestlé all these brands need to be damaged. On the other hand, in my opinion, if sales sink by 10% behaviour begin to change see **Crash on Demand**, later on.

---

45 https://www.thegrocer.co.uk/results/rachels-organic-owner-lactalis-nestle-suffers-11-turnover-drop/649208.article
46 https://www.penguin.co.uk/books/107/1075171/belching-out-the-devil/9780091927042.html
47 https://en.wikipedia.org/wiki/List_of_Nestl%C3%A9_brands

The Algorithmic Anarchist   Hugh Barnard 24/10/21

Brandalism

There's a website for this[48]. Simply, it's the subversion of street advertising by alternative messages. To some extent, because the posters are well-designed and 'arty' people tune these efforts out (we actually interpolate (fill in the gaps) a lot of what we believe we 'see'), a shame. However with some simple home grown gestures, see the **Bullshit Gesture** entry, for example, you can help this very worthy enterprise.

From a point of view of changing dominant narratives, it's important work, see this quote

Paul Mazur, a Wall Street banker working for Lehman Brothers during the great economic slump of the 1930s, is cited as declaring "We must shift America from a needs to a desires-culture. People must be trained to desire, to want new things, even before the old have been entirely consumed. [...] Man's desires must overshadow his needs."

Bullshit Gesture, The

This is part of my personal Brandalism (see the entry) game and communication. Take any common advertising slogan and substitute 'bullshit' at an appropriate point. Here's a couple of examples to get you started. Sky, 'Believe in Better' becomes 'Believe in Bullshit' and Curry's PC World (incidentally, a dreadful place) 'At Curry's PC World We Start with You' becomes 'At Curry's PC World We Start with Bullshit'. See what I mean? It's fun too. Make your own, put them on stickers and t-shirts.

---
48 http://brandalism.ch/

Cash

Use cash whenever you can. You may have seen articles[49] (or trial balloons) saying a pure electronic cash free state would be so much better. It wouldn't, because you could be subject to immediate theft for any transaction, otherwise known as bail-ins and confiscations.

The thieves would not be the 'criminals', they would be the banks and your government. Understand also, the Zero Lower Bound, near zero interest rates that many 'economists' believe is caused partly by issuance of cash. If interest rates are very low or negative (which is only sustainable in a no-cash scenario) then you are trapped, if there is no cash to draw from the bank and spend.

Also, in France (and soon, I believe in the UK, though currently watered down[50]) there is a procedure call ATD[51] which just removes a sum from your bank account (usually to the tax authorities) with minimal justification. Also, extortionate charges by your bank for the 'privilege' of having this inflicted upon you.

Some of the status-quo justifications are that cash is 'expensive' to produce and manage, that it is anonymous and therefore used for tax evasion, drug trafficking and terrorism. However, it is also supports privacy, autonomy, and freedom, probably one of main reasons for disliking it. See also the entry on **Bail In** and **Cashless Society**.

---

49 https://www.theguardian.com/business/2021/jun/16/cashless-society-draws-closer-with-only-one-in-six-payments-now-in-cash
50 https://www.telegraph.co.uk/finance/personalfinance/tax/11244410/George-Osborne-waters-down-plans-to-raid-bank-accounts.html
51 https://droit-finances.commentcamarche.com/contents/1129-saisie-attribution-et-avis-a-tiers-detenteur-definitions

The Algorithmic Anarchist   Hugh Barnard 24/10/21

Cashless Society[52]

This goes with the entry for cash but broadens it. A cashless society is a society of near complete control by (neo-liberal states) private for-profit banks or (traditional 'communist' and totalitarian states) the state itself, directly. Difficult to say which is worse.

Try one or two thought experiments[53], the state has implemented (as in China) social credit[54] and decides your social credit has become negative, so you no longer have access to payment, perhaps for a limited time. Or, more likely in Western society, the bank has some kind of computer problem (looking at you TSB) and you can't pay anyone anything, until the problem is solved.

Effectively, all your day to day economic activity is in the hands of a third party without interests aligned to your well-being. A cardless person, or a person with the 'wrong' card, is also excluded.

In winter 2019, I went to a conference in Amsterdam[55] and I encountered many shops and small restaurants that were 'card only'. Worse, they wouldn't take one of my main, funded cards (issued in the central EU area, France), happily I had a couple of others and, in one case, went elsewhere. So, even for the non-marginalised, such as myself, this is potentially a significant problem.

Alternative and community currencies are an important tool and opportunity for resisting and overcoming this.

---

52 https://en.wikipedia.org/wiki/Cashless_society
53 https://plato.stanford.edu/entries/thought-experiment/
54 https://en.wikipedia.org/wiki/Social_Credit_System
55 https://www.tni.org/en/futureispublic

Citizen Science

We should leave science to scientists, the big corporations, and the government, shouldn't we? Science usually ends up concerning the well being of everyone, nuclear power, drugs, pesticides and pollution to give simple examples. We need to know everything we can about it, to create pressure for informed decisions, to boycott or stop using noxious substances (glyphosate[56] on gardens is an immediate example) and to create data that 'we' own. These are intellectual spaces of autonomy and power.

To go further, we need to participate and build our own technology where possible and *where it may be fun*. Fun is a good motive too. Again, why do that? Simple example, Amazon Alexa and Google Mini, superficially nice but these companies are, in my opinion, abusively dominant and they continuously take data from your private domain. If you want something like this, build it and open source it or use the design that is open sourced.

Second example, pollution sensing. In London, sensors were actually shut down for 'reasons of cost' but actually to mask the extent of the problem[57], only recently revealed. There is no reason to trust government in this area.

---

56 https://en.wikipedia.org/wiki/Glyphosate
57 https://www.theguardian.com/environment/2016/may/17/boris-johnson-held-back-negative-findings-of-air-pollution-report

Third example, the Volkswagen and other faked data scandals[58]. As Bertrand Russell[59] proposed, there is 'knowledge by acquaintance' and 'knowledge by description'. Figures on spreadsheets without access to the original physical testing is 'knowledge by description'. It improves, somewhat, when corroborated from a number of different and preferably neutral sources. But.

Last example, the super sewer[60], enormous costs for the consumer and profits to the water companies was commissioned and build using mathematical models and not using experimental data. Of course, the search for profit was entirely 'another matter', of course.

Cloward–Piven

I'm quoting this straight from Wikipedia but take a look at the original article, '*The two stated that many Americans who were eligible for welfare were not receiving benefits, and that a welfare enrolment drive would strain local budgets, precipitating a crisis at the state and local levels that would be a wake-up call for the federal government*'. Incidentally. The ultimate aim of this strategy was, to quote 't*o wipe out poverty by establishing a guaranteed annual income*', an exceptionally modern concern as of 2020.

My own intuition about this is that this 'overloading' is probably a more general strategy for a more effective and (sometimes) fun engagement with the status quo. The ubiquity and price of computers gives us the tools too. This is an area where we can profitably build **Bots** to do some of the work for us.

---
58 https://www.bbc.co.uk/news/business-34324772
59 https://en.wikipedia.org/wiki/Bertrand_Russell
60 https://www.theguardian.com/uk-news/2016/nov/14/london-super-sewer-is-waste-of-4bn-says-assessor

The Algorithmic Anarchist   Hugh Barnard 24/10/21

When [Asterix goes to Rome](https://en.wikipedia.org/wiki/Asterix_Conquers_Rome)[61], he manages to confuse the bureaucracy there, with a huge set of conflicting demands that eventually the various departments start to echo to one another. It's something like an auto-immune disease for paperwork and procedure. Just sayin'.

To give an example, one of my current projects measures overhead aircraft noise and timing (because the early morning is unpleasant for everyone, for example). However this is easily extended to send complaint emails too. It may be for this reason that many organisations and institutions make their on-line complaint processes very convoluted.

Clutter

This entry is about public realm, but could and can become much, much wider. Our streets are full of signs, do this, don't do that, directions and road markings. As a cyclist my favourites are the little white bicycles that appear to do nothing at all.

Add to this, ubiquitous advertising, some illuminated on bus stops and every other every available space, for our delight. In the UK, add to this the nefarious 'free calls' and Wi-Fi proposed by BT's (and actually Google and others as partners) Inlink[62] which will collect data from you, track you and generally cyber-agress you in exchange for a pathetic amount of 'free stuff'. These things were also used by drug dealers, when introduced. Use the library instead, they'll take some data too, though.

So, our streets are unpleasantly cluttered, apart from from being

---

61 https://en.wikipedia.org/wiki/Asterix_Conquers_Rome
62 https://www.wired.co.uk/article/linkuk-bt-google-free-wifi-and-calls-london

polluted and noisy, they are not places where we would be happy to walk, talk and greet our friends. Grenoble actually removed all street advertising[63] and replaced it with trees.

All this signage and advertising burns a lot of energy unnecessarily too, in the interests of convergence, we could save a bit of the planet and, incidentally, a little cash too.

Co-Creation

My borough is keen on co-creation[64] at the moment. We, the benighted proles are going to co-create useful stuff with the borough in a congenial and collegiate partnership. Indeed, apparently, many services have already been co-created, oh joy!

We see very little of this, however and certainly it doesn't seem to touch the Pareto 80% areas, website actions and navigation, how to contact, how to 'do'. As the cynics who pass me in the garden say "I'm not going to vote because nothing changes".

Worse, we have asymmetric co-creation, to mangle Bill Hicks, 'you are free to co-create what we tell you to'. But none of the co-creation initiatives can find their way (easily or at all) from the bottom of the pile where the benighted proles dwell.

---

63 https://www.goodnewsnetwork.org/europes-first-ad-free-city-replaces-billboards-trees/
64 https://en.wikipedia.org/wiki/Co-creation

The Algorithmic Anarchist   Hugh Barnard 24/10/21

The borough is also using a platform for idea submissions and voting. However apart from the cheery front-end that the proles see, there is also a *back-end* that enables detailed data to be extracted and examined. This part, is of course, not accessible to the ho-polloi who might benefit from some of side products of the analysis.

Colonise

This is part of another 'essay' that I have not (yet) written and may not write. I am using the word in the sense that Henri Lebfevre[65] used it, the colonisation of everyday life, to quote from Wikipedia: *capitalism changed such that everyday life was to be colonized— turned into a zone of sheer consumption.*

Look around at mobile phone use on public transport, every moment is devoted to consuming media, music, video clips, games, and TV shows. The phone remains patiently by the bedside, whilst the consumer struggles with interrupted sleep. If you are not doing this (and I am not) *you are a traitor to consumption* and must do better.

My mantra here is 'divide', 'infantilise' and 'colonise', the three step programme of the new Spectacle, post Debord, an active, toxic and aggressive illusion. However the threat contains also, to a large extent, the seeds of solution, stop consuming, slow consumption and find pastimes that do not involve consumption. For example, find an instrument and play it, rather than consuming music on 'devices'. More radical, indeed, talk to someone rather than phoning them on your smart phone, turn it off (although it won't really be 'off', see **Blinding**).

---

65 https://en.wikipedia.org/wiki/Henri_Lefebvre

The Algorithmic Anarchist   Hugh Barnard 24/10/21

Incidentally, the current government has been closing a lot of libraries (see also the **Library 451** essay, later on), obviously, libraries are free at the point of use and they compete with the coffee shops. Garden fruit and blackberries compete with the supermarkets, got to stop all that, clearly. Lefebvre is good on public space and invented the idea of the 'right to the city'[66] too.

Competition

Have you noticed that the dominant societal narrative is one of competition? When watching TV, I always think of Highlander, *there can only be one* and of narratives of *austerity* that are designed to make us fight like starving rats.

Strictly Come Dancing, The Apprentice, The Great British Bake Off, Storage Hunters and nearly every quiz show have 'winners' and 'losers' and no elements of cooperation.

Indeed, it is interesting, that there were apparently one or two attempts to make Rollerball[67], a 'real' game just after the release of the original film. Now, at time of writing, some Russian 'entrepreneurs' are planning to make a real-life version of the Hunger Games to take place in Siberia. Go figure.

---

66 https://en.wikipedia.org/wiki/Right_to_the_city
67 https://en.wikipedia.org/wiki/Rollerball_(1975_film)

The Algorithmic Anarchist		Hugh Barnard 24/10/21

Consciousness-Raising[68]

Someone mentioned this to me recently with the wry 'remember that?' tacked on the end. Yes I do, making people aware of stuff. Also, pushing things up an agenda. In terms of anarchist theory, there is often no general agenda though, and quite right too.

So Brandalism, Pranksterism and associated form a web of consciousness raising, the principal agenda being 'there is something else' (but we are not currently sure what it is) or, as Morrison of the Doors sang 'break on through to the other side'. Actually, I'm afraid of definitive agendas and Value Monism[69], it's better, in my opinion, to have rough goals and be iterative.

Also, see look at 'prefiguration[70]' to quote Wikipedia 'Prefigurative politics are the modes of organization and social relationships that strive to reflect the future society being sought by the group. According to Carl Boggs, who coined the term, the desire is to embody "within the ongoing political practice of a movement'.

---

68 https://en.wikipedia.org/wiki/Consciousness_raising
69 https://plato.stanford.edu/entries/value-theory/#Mon
70 https://en.wikipedia.org/wiki/Prefigurative_politics

The Algorithmic Anarchist   Hugh Barnard 24/10/21

Consultations

I've nearly given up replying to consultations, since they are immediately ignored, by whoever. Sometime there's some extra fun and an opportunity for the 'they' to patronise the 'us' in focus groups and workshops. If they have sandwiches, I go, it's a free (but small) meal, if there are only biscuits, I avoid.

However, if one is feeling ranty and has a little spare time, they do offer the opportunity for some fun though. As elsewhere, I prefer humour to opposition as a clearer way of showing my feelings. Strong negative emotions are continued engagement with the status quo and an additional reason for them to ignore you. The objective is to ignore it, let it die and create something else.

I call some of the worst of these things 'insultations'. We invite you, we pretend to listen and then we do something else entirely.

Cooperation

I enjoy and admire Kropotkin, Mutual Aid[71], another phrase for the idea. We are sold competition because it divides us and creates artificial scarcity, but our natural state is also equally cooperative.

Some of the conceptual mistakes about this, come from Carnegie's hijacking of Herbert Spencer[72] (thence to Darwin). However it is difficult to distinguish the 'mistakes' and the edifice of propaganda, that, latterly the Atlas Network[73] and others have built up.

---

71 https://theanarchistlibrary.org/library/petr-kropotkin-mutual-aid-a-factor-of-evolution
72 https://plato.stanford.edu/entries/spencer/
73 https://www.atlasnetwork.org/

Crash on Demand

This is a good idea sketched out here, by David Holgrem Crash on Demand[74]. The core idea is for the middle classes (and preferably 'everyone') to start reducing consumption by about 10% and crash the whole 'spend to keep the economy (aka the neo-liberal economy, debt and consumption) alive. This is, to some extent, 'broad boycott' or 'political minimalism'.

In fact, in the early part of the COVID pandemic, this idea had a decent field test and it worked pretty well, stuff closed and went bankrupt. However, it was also a shotgun effect, a better idea is to start consciously choosing the companies and platforms that need to close. Looking at you, Facebook, for a start.

Credit

Part of the neo-liberal project aka **The System** is poor wages and use of credit, rather than decent wages and saving. Poor wages and ensuing credit[75] are tools of control, artificial scarcity and profit. Why with central bank rates, just above zero, card companies, usually American owned can charge 87%! Oh joy!

Same for the predatory lenders that advertise heavily on television, all rates of nearly 100% or 'only £5 per month' to borrow £100. People on poor wages or Universal Credit are often pushed into these loans to eat or pay rent too.

See below on Credit Cards too.

---

74 https://holmgren.com.au/wp-content/uploads/2014/01/Crash-on-demand.pdf
75 https://talkpoverty.org/2019/02/25/credit-card-debt-poverty-predatory-lending/ (anecdotal but useful)

The Algorithmic Anarchist   Hugh Barnard 24/10/21

Credit Cards

If you can live without credit cards, do so. I keep one because of the extra protection offered for travel, but I rarely use it. Issuers will re-use and sell your data. So, if you can't afford it, don't buy it or save until you can afford it. Debt is social control and slavery. This is also part of what I call **Blinding**, see that entry.

Cryptocurrency

No, no. I'm in favour of alternative currencies and, pace Lietaer[76], an eco-system of currencies for different purposes, but not in favour of large scale crypto, of which Bitcoin[77] is the oldest and most obvious example. First, we may not want 'algorithmic trust' in our lives and may want human trust instead. Second, the question of scale, large leads to the absent owner problem and the current set of destructive distortions in our current economy.

I don't actually believe that the technology is particularly innovative and also, proof of work[78] (not all cryptocurrencies do this continuously) wastes a great deal of energy.

There's also, currently (2019) a lot of over-promotion and possibly outright fraud attached to the area, see for example OneCoin[79] and Tether.

---

76 https://en.wikipedia.org/wiki/Bernard_Lietaer
77 https://en.wikipedia.org/wiki/Bitcoin
78 https://en.wikipedia.org/wiki/Proof_of_work
79 https://en.wikipedia.org/wiki/OneCoin

Delete Me

You may not have noticed how difficult it is to be removed from a website, once you have 'registered' on a website. In two recent cases, and both (to their shame) are UK non-profits, I have had to threaten them with the Information Commissioner and I am still not sure whether my details have actually been removed. People lie and patronise[80] once they have put on their 'work clothes' and set their alienation to a maximum value of 11.

So, insist on being deleted from things that you have finished with.

Demonstrations

Younger, I used to go on demonstrations, Campaign for Nuclear Disarmament (CND) mainly. Now, I do not. I believe that peaceful demonstrations are ignored or (like petitions, see the entry) are, indeed, useful because they blow off a little steam.

Then, in the case of more lively demonstrations, the demonstrators are kettled, photographed, infiltrated and, if the demonstration is successful, the images are suppressed as much as possible by the BBC and all other bits of mainstream media. If anything material happens to get broken, the headlines read 'Anarchy Rules'. Of course, in a very real way, we wish that it did.

Finally, of course, we show our hand. To be Machiavellian (for a moment), it's probably much more disturbing for the status quo to have a very limited understanding of any radical aims. Keep them guessing, that's fun as well.

---

80 https://www.penguin.co.uk/books/110/1107904/i-you-we-them/9780099592372.html

Depave

This is part of the general gardening and food thread. In London, an enormous area of soil is paved, usually in gardens and used for parking or, simply, to avoid maintaining the green space. This is one of the 'alienating' effects of a system that is designed to make us more and more, time-poor. All this space is useful for fruit trees, bushes and easy-to-grow vegetables.

There are (at least) two other problems associated with this paving, flash flooding and heat island[81] effect. Since a great deal of the paving will not let the water through or out, the water will flow over it, when there's enough there'll be an extra flood of some kind because there's no escape route. All cities and large towns are like storage heaters (which usually contain bricks, that's a clue, isn't it?), so extra concrete, tarmac or paving stones add to this effect.

Finally which would you prefer, some greenery or some concrete[82]? These are small areas that are under your control, use them well.

There's a movement that started in Portland OR, called Depave.org[83].

---

81 https://en.wikipedia.org/wiki/Urban_heat_island
82 https://www.newscientist.com/article/mg24933270-800-green-spaces-arent-just-for-nature-they-boost-our-mental-health-too/
83 https://depave.org/

Echo Chamber

Even though we try, we live in sets of echo chambers. I include myself in this. Why, social media encourages and builds them, via a recommender[84]. When Twitter suggests 'who to follow' they will often be somebody who shares your interests or political leanings, certainly not serendipitous, random or diametrically opposed to your thinking. These are small world networks[85] in graph theory[86] putting you into a comfortable clique.

Outside social media, most of academia doesn't reach outside into the world[87]. For science and technology, there is long convoluted process of discovery, journal articles, (often) patents and commercialisation, see **Open Everything**.

However, the knowledge and dialogue remains embedded and hidden, in for-profit journals and denied (especially to the developing world) via patenting and other commercial restrictions. In the third sector, same thing, especially now that the bigger charities have decided they have overpaid CEOs.

To be aphoristic, 'the only person listening to you is you'. This theme is continued somewhat in 'reaching out' and 'reaching down'.

---

84 https://en.wikipedia.org/wiki/Recommender_system
85 https://en.wikipedia.org/wiki/Small-world_network
86 https://en.wikipedia.org/wiki/Graph_theory
87 https://www.ukri.org/councils/esrc/impact-toolkit-for-economic-and-social-sciences/defining-impact/ (or not)

The Algorithmic Anarchist   Hugh Barnard 24/10/21

Encryption

As I write the the UK Investigatory Powers Act 2016[88] has just become law, as the Guardian said 'without a whimper'. This gives a lot of extra authority for bulk data collection, for example, logs of your internet surfing and logs of mobile phone calls. It's worth saying that a great many specialist feel that this blanket approach is near useless (because there's too much, even for statistical methods) and somewhat dangerous, needles and haystacks.

So, the main objective may be just to oppress and dampen dissent. Also, as I write, someone if France has just been imprisoned for 'repeatedly surfing Islamic State material', in fact for Orwell's 'thoughtcrime'[89]. As an aside, I have had the intuition, from time to time, in the last 20 years that the Civil Service and government have begun to use 1984 as a manual rather than a novel, witness the names of departments, Ofwat, Ofgem etc. I'm waiting for MiniLove to replace the Ministry of Justice now. Enough already.

There are two other entries in this document that relate to this, **Friction** and **Public Key Encryption**. Encryption via the padlocky thing is becoming standard but will only give partial protection from mass surveillance logs and there are limits and holes. So the 'best' way to surf may be (see the article) via Tor[90] which will anonymise to some extent and 'create friction'.

---

88 https://en.wikipedia.org/wiki/Investigatory_Powers_Act_2016
89 https://en.wikipedia.org/wiki/Thoughtcrime
90 https://en.wikipedia.org/wiki/Tor_(network)

The Algorithmic Anarchist   Hugh Barnard 24/10/21

Unhappily, the best way to use email is to pay for a privacy oriented provider such as Protonmail[91] (other brands are available) rather than the major 'free' providers, Google, Hotmail and Yahoo. I certainly wouldn't use Yahoo, anyway. Remember, *if it is free, then you are the product.*

All this is very partial, but currently I'm concentrating my own efforts on the two major cyber activities in my life, email and the web as a project of steady and progressive improvement. I'm not currently a 'smart' phone user and have a few words to say about **Android**, see the entry. Also, a certain amount of privacy work is proportionate. If you are seeking personal modesty, the requirement is lower than if you are a whistle-blower, for example.

Energy

A great of the thinking in this text concerns 'liberating' or 'unanchoring' the bottom two tiers of Maslow's hierarchy of needs (qv). That is, roughly, an abundance of food, shelter, warmth and safety for *everyone*. I'm, personally, not too worried about knick-knacks, but opinions vary.

A small (true) story about this. In an un-named small South East Asian nation, the powers-that-be decided that a small corner of native population needed 'progress'.

So they moved them out of their villages into tower blocks with bathrooms and running water. So far, so good. But, also, in doing so they could no longer keep chickens, maybe some goats or grow a few vegetables on their garden patches.

---

91 https://protonmail.com/

The Algorithmic Anarchist   Hugh Barnard 24/10/21

Also any surrounding tropical fruit trees that could be foraged were cut down, to protect the foundations of the tower blocks. Of course, now they had moved from partial self-sufficiency to dependency, for food, power bills, water bills.

Thus, they were integrated into modern society and their lives were more hygienic and 'better'. Actually, what happened is that they were plugged fully into the modern economic system and thus 'under control'. I do not believe that this was done consciously, certainly the population did not represent a physical threat, except perhaps in the sense that their manner of living presented an alternative and prefigurative[92] narrative, divorced from the central one.

So, back to the subject, energy and power. There is now a great deal of possibility for change in the use of solar energy with increasingly efficient battery storage. We need the batteries as well, before we can abandon the National Grid and the power companies. Also, we need to develop micro-grids[93] to provide a little resiliency and mutual support within neighbourhoods.

Wind is somewhat problematic in an urban setting and useful as part of turbine co-operative and mutuals where there's some open space.

It's worth considering simple, passive solutions too (back to the future, I started thinking about this in about 1971). For example, Trombe walls[94] seem to have been neglected and are fairly easy to retrofit.

---

92 https://en.wikipedia.org/wiki/Prefigurative_politics
93 https://en.wikipedia.org/wiki/Microgrid
94 https://en.wikipedia.org/wiki/Trombe_wall

Engagement

Another 21st Orwellian Newspeak[95] word. Our council has 'engagement officers' a sure sign of their confused attitude to their citizens. Truly engaged organisations do not need the word or have specific officers for the activity, they *engage*, rather than having superficially attractive funnels that prevent anything of substance from happening.

Any engagement must sit in the actual departments that *do*, not in some intermediate abstraction. Incidentally this argument is analogous to Up The Organisation[96]'s advice to fire the whole of HR.

Engagement usually ends up as being the *right sort of engagement*, where it's not particularly radical, a little woke and *there's a grant for that*. The grant thing is usually important because it's a tool for control and gatekeeping.

As of this 2021 (plague) year, I've spent about £50 of *my own money* on some fruit bushes for public consumption. No photo-ops, no grant application, no official engagement. Own initiative, even on this microscopic level is good anarchism as middle class infrapolitics[97].

---

95 https://en.wikipedia.org/wiki/Newspeak
96 https://www.goodreads.com/en/book/show/546936.Up_the_Organization
97 https://en.wikipedia.org/wiki/James_C._Scott

The Algorithmic Anarchist   Hugh Barnard 24/10/21

Facebook

I deleted myself from Facebook about five years ago. I'd suggest that anyone do the same, see #DeleteFacebook. Also see my commentary about LinkedIn, if everyone removed themselves from some of these mega-platforms, *they are not worth anything to their shareholders* and have less influence in all our affairs.

At time of writing there was a discussion about buying Twitter via crowdfunding. This collapsed, later on. Depending on organisation and governance, this may very well be a healthier model, or we should just move to Mastodon[98] en mass?

Fair Value

I quote from recent 'accounting standards':

Fundamental to FRS 102 is the concept of 'Fair Value'. Fair value is the amount for which an asset, liability or equity instrument could be exchanged or settled between knowledgeable, willing parties in an arms length transaction. In some instances you may require expert advice to determine a fair value.

Let's analyse a little, *knowledgeable* is to hard to judge, already, *willing* also, when stuff changes hands, especially public or semi-property, there's usually underlying pressure of some kind. As for arms length, well, most of the exchangers and settlers are finance industry or related to it, developers or hedge funds for example.

In transactions involving the sale of public assets, considering a

---

98 https://joinmastodon.org/

recent sell-on in my area (bought £12m, sold on £60m[99]) no-one is apparently very *knowledgeable* or has taken *expert advice*. At the other end of the scale, assets are sometimes sold cheaply to 'friends' of a council. This is also related to the cousin concept of Best Value, which I haven't given a separate entry to:

Therefore, while the message was unequivocally that Compulsory Competitive Tendering was to be withdrawn, the replacement was to be less prescribed, with the intention that local authorities follow a responsive and locally determined method of service provision within a centrally defined framework. Best Value was not, therefore, about what local authorities should do: it was a framework that prescribed how they should decide what to do.

So both these ideas are vague in the extreme. In terms of selling off the family silver, there is (usually) no further investigation above price, monetary amount, as above. For example, in the case of the Network Rail arches[100], sold to 'property management' companies (the Arch Company, backed by Blackstone and Telereal Trillium), will almost certainly result in unaffordable rent increases. Therefore loss of local economic activity to bigger companies, well-being and (keeping being hard headed) economic multipliers[101].

Of course, the counter argument is 'jobs', but these are bullshit jobs[102] not the autonomous, freelance activity that they replaced.

---

99 https://www.theguardian.com/artanddesign/2021/aug/02/msg-sphere-stratford-london-orb-madison-square-gardens
100 https://www.theguardian.com/business/2019/sep/13/network-rail-failed-railway-arch-tenants-in-15bn-sale-say-mps
101 https://www.economicsonline.co.uk/Managing_the_economy/The_multiplier_effect.html
102 https://en.wikipedia.org/wiki/Bullshit_Jobs

The Algorithmic Anarchist   Hugh Barnard 24/10/21

FAQ

Stands for Frequently Asked Questions[103]. This idea has been around probably since the 1980s at the start of a more general use of the internet and mailing lists. However, to quote Wikipedia: *While the name may be recent, the FAQ format itself is quite old. For example, Matthew Hopkins[104] wrote The Discovery of Witches in 1648 as a list of questions and answers, introduced as "Certain Queries answered".* This is the FAQ for this document.

1. Why is some of this, jokey? "If I can't dance, I don't want to be part of your revolution" - Emma Goldman[105] (probably).

2. Why is technical stuff treated non-technically? I want this to be as accessible as possible, even though a lot of the content is 'technical'.

3. I have a question, comment, correction and/or criticism? That isn't really a question, but write to me and I'll try (if I agree) to incorporate it into the next iteration.

4. *Why are there so many footnotes*? This is a sourcebook, so it needs to signal onward destinations. As it exists in a print version, simply putting in-text hyperlinks isn't enough.

5. Why is there 'generous' blank space in this book? For your voluminous notes. You are entirely welcome.

---

103 https://en.wikipedia.org/wiki/FAQ
104 https://en.wikipedia.org/wiki/Matthew_Hopkins (see Witchfinder General, too, great film)
105 https://en.wikipedia.org/wiki/Emma_Goldman

The Algorithmic Anarchist		Hugh Barnard 24/10/21

Federation

The only way that 'small things' may become 'loosely joined' (footnote is to book title)[106] is to federate them. There are lots of interesting technical, governance and organisational problems to solve when doing this too.

However 'big things', especially big organisations become distant, monolithic and unaccountable, this is Nicholas Albery's[107] 'law of scale' but there's probably some detailed science about this somewhere or other. Meanwhile, look at government, IBM, Google, Facebook and Microsoft and take my word for it, for the moment.

Connected with the idea or ideal of the small is Subsidiarity[108], the principle of deciding and acting at the lowest possible level. Actually this is baked into the EU[109], but they (and national governments) tend to conveniently forget it, it's always simpler to act from the centre, pushing down.

Besides, those 'local communities' (that incessantly repeated patronising appellation) can't really be trusted, can they?

---

106 https://www.goodreads.com/book/show/753804.Small_Pieces_Loosely_Joined
107 https://en.wikipedia.org/wiki/Nicholas_Albery
108 https://en.wikipedia.org/wiki/Subsidiarity
109 https://eur-lex.europa.eu/summary/glossary/subsidiarity.html

The Algorithmic Anarchist   Hugh Barnard 24/10/21

Free Software

Stallman[110]: The two terms describe almost the same category of software, but they stand for views based on fundamentally different values. Open source[111] is a development methodology; free software[112] is a social movement."

Different values? Yes. But not mutually exclusive. Rather than aligning with one or the other, many people find varying degrees of resonance with the values underlying each term.

I lean to the Free Software side, but also consider FOSS[113], Free and Open Source, squaring the circle.

Friction

This is an an enlargement of the Cloward-Piven[114] and Encryption entry. Every little bit of friction with regard to the status-quo is useful. Some examples are, refusal to use on-line resources, paying with a cheque-book (if you still have one), writing snail-mail letters, refusing to give your mobile number, and, in general, choosing the most inconvenient method for the authorities and banks etc.

---

110 https://en.wikipedia.org/wiki/Richard_Stallman
111 https://en.wikipedia.org/wiki/Open_source
112 https://en.wikipedia.org/wiki/Free_software
113 https://en.wikipedia.org/wiki/Free_and_open-source_software
114 https://en.wikipedia.org/wiki/Cloward%E2%80%93Piven_strategy

This also applies to **Encryption**, for which there's a separate entry. Encryption will not necessarily prevent a person or organisation from breaking into your affairs, since it can be broken (at a certain strength) or keys can be revealed or stolen. However, everything that is encrypted, just makes the work harder.

Incidentally, a number of intelligence analysts have already stated that mass surveillance is often an obstacle to preventing terrorism, since there's too much data presented, needles and haystacks.

If you have a valid complaint then complain, often and remorselessly through official channels too, it's fun, make sure that it's polite and not vexatious. That is, don't give them ammunition regarding replies.

Gardening

Yes, gardening! Especially fruit, vegetables and all kinds of edibles. There are three 'theory' strands to this.

The first one is (if you will) a Marxist one about the sale of labour and why we are obliged to do this. We sell our labour for warmth, shelter and food. We can survive, somewhat unhappily, without a great deal of the rest. I am not a huge fan of Zerzan[115] (or any of the other anarcho-primitivists) for example, but see the section on **Guerilla Gardening**.

---

115 https://en.wikipedia.org/wiki/John_Zerzan

However, when the working classes left the countryside for the cities (either via enclosure[116], poverty, or during industrial revolution for example) they also left behind the possibility of feeding themselves, either partially or wholly without capitalist style, sale of labour. Gardening, guerilla gardening and foraging can partially restore that. In an ideal world, micro-economies of local exchange (my carrots for your potatoes) can augment the effect too.

I have covered the second one in **Import Substitution** (I've misused the phrase somewhat), anything grown or foraged is not being bought from the supermarkets, so their power diminishes. Always a good thing.

Last, trees, bushes, and greenery in general make the city a more pleasant place (observable mental health effects[117]), over and above planters and tree-in-a-box tokens that our putative lords and masters plant, hoping to sell these as 'greening' or with some radical improvement.

---

116 https://en.wikipedia.org/wiki/Enclosure
117 https://nhsforest.org/evidence-benefits

The Algorithmic Anarchist   Hugh Barnard 24/10/21

Generosity

This is a central part of an (left-leaning or I prefer human-leaning, if you will) anarchist economy. Of course, the diametric opposite, selfishness as rationality, appears centrally in Ayn Rand[118] and more recently in some forms of techno-libertarianism. I am positing Kropotkin[119], for example.

In neo-liberal world, a transaction is a closed loop, I give you money and you give me something and there the matter (probably) ends. Better is that we continue, over the months and years, as the relationship with a small shop or market stall, but not 'big anonymous supermarket with self checkouts'. That means that there is a human component in the transaction too. Last week I had an extra croissant, because they were a bit squashed. The system(s) in any large shop or supermarket do not allow for this behaviour.

Up, another notch, from this, are pay-it-forward[120] systems. Simply, you ask the person to whom you gave something to do (or give) something for someone else, so that there is an open ripple of giving or doing in a localised part of society. As good anarchists they can choose a) to do so, or not b) choose what to do or give. It is up to you and then up to them.

Finally, there is pure altruism, you give/do without any speech act or expectation. I'm not bothering with the Kantian purity of the act, with luck, the main effects are existential and beneficial. Also, even this isn't really pure, it may make you feel good or optimistic. My advice concerning that is 'enjoy', enough already.

---
118 https://en.wikipedia.org/wiki/Ayn_Rand
119 https://en.wikipedia.org/wiki/Peter_Kropotkin
120 https://en.wikipedia.org/wiki/Pay_it_forward

The Algorithmic Anarchist   Hugh Barnard 24/10/21

GPS

Global Positioning System. Switch it off, if it's in your mobile phone (it is, if it is a 'smart phone'), this is part of **Blinding** too. If something or a web site asks you to *share your location* be like Nancy Reagan and 'just say no', unless you really, really need it. Then switch it off 'afterwards'.

Note that it may not actually be off[121], especially in Android phones.

Grant Funding

In principle, I am 'against' grant funding, from whatever source. Here are some of the reasons

1. In general, funds are allocated via 'competition' judged by 'experts' on a basis of created and artificial scarcity. I'm not against 'expertise', especially in technical subjects, medicine, aeronautical engineering, and mathematics, for example. However, expertise in badly-defined local matters, for example, belongs to people who live in, and around, the locality.

2. Box ticking, inflexibility and narrowness of focus. Money that 'would have been' useful, if it had been used for an allied subject or activity. One example, from ten years ago, was teaching word processing to people who had little use for it. However, they did have a use for email, since they were older people with families who lived abroad. Of course, the solution was to teach them about email surreptitiously, see point 3.

---

[121] https://www.theverge.com/21401280/android-101-location-tracking-history-stop-how-to

The Algorithmic Anarchist	Hugh Barnard 24/10/21

3. There's a certain kind of systematic dishonesty that goes with reporting for grant funding. It reminds me of a joke (about 1982) from the (then) communist bloc, 'We pretend to work and they pretend to pay us'. So the system gets more and more skewed, via inaccurate feedback, towards the wrong goals. For those who are good at this game, attendance, outputs, and outcomes[122] are often overstated too, a 'good' session will be found to contain about three demoralised attendees.

4. It favours the slick and well resourced, those with the grinning, diverse brochures that tell a great many lies about their activities. Normally these same people pay and treat their staff rather badly as well or (mis)use 'volunteers'. There's often a great deal of cognitive dissonance between the brochure and the organisation.

5. Grants distort and damage any sustainability and autonomy within the organisation's activities and economy. For example, a great deal of grant money flows in, people are hired and equipment purchased, money spent and there are lay-offs and the equipment lies idle. Unnatural peaks and troughs.

6. Grants provides a false ownership, virtue signalling and spurious photo-opportunities for local councillors and (worse) corporates. The corporates are usually trying to mask 'bad' activities by giving a few crumbs to something 'good'. It doesn't really work that way does it? From a text in one of the major 12 Step Programs[123], 'We are self-supporting, refusing all outside contributions'. Enough said.

---

122 https://lmcourse.ces.uwex.edu/Module_1_pages/M1_Section2/HTML/m1s2p3a.htm
123 https://en.wikipedia.org/wiki/Twelve-step_program

Guerilla Gardening[124]

I could make the claim that Winstanley[125] was the first guerilla gardener. Reclaiming neglected plots and planting pretty flowers is part of it, but not the whole, see the **Artwashing** entry. Better to plant or 'encourage' some extra food production too, for reasons I've outlined elsewhere.

Here are three more powerful reasons for taking an interest in food-oriented guerilla gardening too.

1. Free or nearly free (a Marxist would argue (rightly) that labour has gone into it) food is an affront to a system where everything has a monetary value and nothing is 'free'. This is a reason to forage, also.

2. This is the basis for a 'generosity' component in a very flawed economy. Generosity is a pay-it-forward[126] component whereas transactions are closed-loop. Generosity is political act, too.

3. Prefiguration[127]. Starting to live within a partial framework of the society that you would like to see and live in.

---

124 https://en.wikipedia.org/wiki/Guerrilla_gardening
125 https://en.wikipedia.org/wiki/Gerrard_Winstanley
126 https://en.wikipedia.org/wiki/Pay_it_forward
127 https://en.wikipedia.org/wiki/Prefigurative_politics

Hackathon

Beware the humble hackathon[128][129], my friends. As the cartoon said, 'We give them beer and pizza, lock them away for 12 hours, and they give us $1m ideas'. So, a great many of these, especially when run by corporate entities (using slogans such as 'open', 'help save the planet' etc. etc.) are anything but[130].

Like a great deal of 'volunteering' (I still do some, but only for small, near-autonomous organisations, where at all possible) this is slavery or co-optation.

Before deciding whether to participate, examine the organisation and examine the software licence (if that is what the given hackathon does) of the product or project that is to be hacked. Also see the entry on **API**s and the illusion of 'openness'.

---

128 https://en.wikipedia.org/wiki/Hackathon
129 https://www.poetryfoundation.org/poems/42916/jabberwocky (Haha!)
130 https://www.wired.com/story/sociologists-examine-hackathons-and-see-exploitation/

The Algorithmic Anarchist   Hugh Barnard 24/10/21

Hierarchy of Evil

This is a mental tool and thought experiment that I use for 'partial activism'. Here is my ranking of supermarkets, as an easy example. My ratings are, of course, subject to debate, but it's important to think about this, then punish and reward.

Name	Rating 2019	Rating 2021	Notes
Cooperative	8	8	If possible
Waitrose	7	7	Expensive though
Marks & Spencer	6	6	
Morrison	5	0	Private equity now
Tesco	3	3	
ASDA	0	3	Walmart sold it

I try to buy as much as I can from street traders and markets now. But this requires contact with other human beings, very healthy but difficult, perhaps, for the 24-hour-screen generation and COVID.

This approach can be applied to all other 'sources of supply' too, I now buy books, as much as I can, from Hive. Amazon are often cheaper but the result is (I have a friend who is a novelist) that the author receives much less, they avoid taxes and their working environment is horrible. I haven't used just one value for choosing and ranking, there's usually a cluster, I am usually unhappy with (what philosophers call) Value Monism[131].

---

131 https://plato.stanford.edu/entries/value-theory/#Mon

It is up to individuals (especially if they regards themselves as individualist anarchists, I am not) to make their own hierarchies and, perhaps, explain them or suggest them to others. If there is broad agreement, everything moves in one direction and the results are significant. See the entry on **Consciousness Raising** too, an old idea that needs to come around again.

Hieroglyphics

I was originally thinking about learning some Linear B[132] or other hieroglyphic text, as a way of expressing political ideas in a more amusing form of graffiti. I have not completely abandoned this idea.

However, Linear B is syllabic, I've been thinking about obscure and alphabetic recently, I think that Noto Sans Shavian[133] may 'do'.

Hipsters[134]

Some of my friends chide me for my dislike of hipsters.

My feeling is this, they are one of the first youth trends to be pure spectacular (in the Debordian[135] sense), recuperated rebellion. With regard to core ethics or philosophy, it seems vacuous or consumption-driven. As long as they can get organic oils for their beards, lumberjack shirts, iPhones, iMacs, and skinny jeans, they will be perfectly content.

---

132 https://omniglot.com/writing/linearb.htm
133 https://fonts.google.com/noto/specimen/Noto+Sans+Shavian?noto.query=shavian
134 https://en.wikipedia.org/wiki/Hipster_(contemporary_subculture)
135 https://en.wikipedia.org/wiki/Guy_Debord

The Algorithmic Anarchist   Hugh Barnard 24/10/21

They represent the (temporary, I hope) defeat of youth as an agency or focus for radical change. This, of course, I accept is also a cruel generalisation, there must be some good ones, however I do not have the patience to go down to Hoxton and conduct interviews to find them.

I feel it is somewhat up to we, grumpy, vaguely and naively 1960s radicalised, to start making some changes now[136].

Import Substitution

I've misused the term import substitution[137], for individual/local substitution, rather than national and trade theory heavy. My view is that in the a 'path' (there isn't just one path) towards anarchy, it is a valid concept for smaller groups, not just for nation states.

For example, when you start to grow or to forage some of diet, this is 'source substitution' with regard to supermarkets and (sadly) towards market stalls. Let's take another, if you start a local, cash only (at point of exchange) 'eBay', you have substituted or partially substituted for eBay, itself. Take a look at *fairmondo*[138] for example.

Do not worry about partial substitution, this is a step in the right direction. Even a single carrot *not bought from Tesco is a nano-revolution*. This is also related to Scott's[139] idea of infrapolitics. I re-discuss this under the entry **Absolutes**.

---
136 Alfred North Whitehead used the phrase **great refusal** for the determination not to succumb to the facticity of things as they are—to favour instead the imagination of the ideal
137 https://en.wikipedia.org/wiki/Import_substitution_industrialization
138 https://www.fairmondo.de/global
139 https://en.wikipedia.org/wiki/James_C._Scott

The Algorithmic Anarchist   Hugh Barnard 24/10/21

Industry

I'm gradually collecting a list of things that are not 'industries'. The most obvious is the 'finance industry', just a load of people (including myself, two decades ago) sitting in front of screens juggling numbers. I need a complete essay on 'full reserve banking[140]' (one of the approaches) and 'thin finance[141]' that I may, or may not have time to write. For example, I do believe in simple futures[142] as they smooth out difficulties for cash crop farming.

The second candidate, is, of course, the advertising 'industry', with finance, one of the root causes of our modern ills and now ubiquitous and embedded in everything. Even our dear smartphones, that we (you, not me) prize so dearly are a vector, for selling stuff in the pauses between using them for consuming stuff, that is. Two excellent simple (and proposed by multiple sources) remedies, the Robin Hood Tax[143] and an advertising tax[144]. We can work something out for public service advertising.

I will not even mention[145] soft drinks 'industry' or the public relations 'industry'. Kensucky Fracked Chicken, anyone?

---

140 https://en.wikipedia.org/wiki/Full-reserve_banking
141 Finance without complex financial derivatives, commodity futures only, for example.
142 https://en.wikipedia.org/wiki/Futures_contract
143 https://en.wikipedia.org/wiki/Robin_Hood_tax
144 https://en.wikipedia.org/wiki/Criticism_of_advertising#Taxation_as_revenue_and_control
145 https://en.wikipedia.org/wiki/Apophasis

The Algorithmic Anarchist   Hugh Barnard 24/10/21

Interstitial

If Nicholas Negroponte called a book, a good while ago now, Being Digital[146], I would call some of this 'Being Interstitial'. In this, my view is somewhat similar to some autonomists, for example John Holloway of Crack Capitalism[147], but I am probably less romantic, more networked and more modest in ambition.

However, 'weeds grow in the cracks' and so do fruit and vegetables. The 'other' problem for which Holloway has been heavily criticised is the difference between individual acts of autonomy and the more collective acts that rock the whole system. Almost certainly, some of the answer is networking in the cyber sense, this being why any government takes such an interest in our mobile telephone logs, browsing logs, and any other citizen **Metadata**[148] that they can lay their little hands on. They do not want to see things that are 'clumping up' (aka 'trending', hence tight control of 'trends') as a precursor to becoming something antagonistic and perhaps even challenging for them.

Terrorism is a glib explanation, but we are certainly a target. In a sense, this is hopeful, they are realistic enough to be afraid of (some of) us[149].

---

146 https://en.wikipedia.org/wiki/Being_Digital
147 https://en.wikipedia.org/wiki/Crack_Capitalism
148 https://en.wikipedia.org/wiki/Metadata
149 https://en.wikipedia.org/wiki/V_for_Vendetta_(film)

The Algorithmic Anarchist   Hugh Barnard 24/10/21

Kulaks

Kulaks[150] were were smallholders, autonomous and often producing a saleable surplus in Russia. They were criticised by Lenin and decimated by Stalin[151]. This is used by the right to show the dangers of 'communism', as defined by the right. In fact, it shows the dangers of dictatorship, (any kind of collectivisation) as a project and the false belief that scale and uniformity lead to 'efficiency'. Why have I chosen to talk about this?

From the right, we have the mega-corporations who will, via abuse of dominant positions, squash or suborn (Amazon 'marketplace', Facebook, eBay etc.) most small businesses. Also from the UK government, presumably irritated by feeble agitations of *actual* freely negotiated contracts for labour, we have IR35[152]. We have, instead, the gig economy, a modern form of slavery.

From the conventional left (at the end of 2019, during an election period) we have large scale nationalisation, collective state-owned uniformity as panacea. There's a case to be made for some natural monopolies, but the governance and ownership may have much better models (Coops and CICs[153], for example).

Small scale enterprise and genuine skills-for-hire (as opposed to employee contracts for 'roles' that one is obliged to be 'passionate' about) are being squeezed from either side of the conventional political spectrum. Personal and small scale autonomy must not stand, too dangerous for all the vested interests of the status quo.

---

150 https://en.wikipedia.org/wiki/Kulak
151 https://en.wikipedia.org/wiki/Dekulakization
152 https://en.wikipedia.org/wiki/IR35
153 https://en.wikipedia.org/wiki/Community_interest_company

The Algorithmic Anarchist   Hugh Barnard 24/10/21

Linux

This is a piece of zero-cost software that will run your computer as well as Windows. Better still it will perform well on 'older' computers so they need not be thrown away and can be re-purposed, donated and generally have their lifetimes prolonged.

The energy and ecological cost of building a 'new' computer (or indeed smart phone) is enormous and throwing away the old one[154] and one of the only (invalid) reasons for having a new one is new versions of Windows, increased bloat[155]. This is a game that IBM allegedly used to play with mainframes in the 1980s, bigger software equals more memory to be sold or rented, especially if you don't let others into the market[156].

Linux is free, but you will have to learn some new ways of thinking, never a bad thing. I have used Linux as my main desktop computer since 2007. Currently I use and recommend Linux Mint[157]. See the entry on **Open Source** too.

_____

154 https://www.theatlantic.com/technology/archive/2016/09/the-global-cost-of-electronic-waste/502019/
155 We've gone from 640K (DOS) to about 6.08GB
156 https://www.nytimes.com/1973/09/18/archives/ibm-is-found-guilty-in-antitrust-suit-and-told-to-pay-telex.html
157 https://linuxmint.com/

The Algorithmic Anarchist   Hugh Barnard 24/10/21

Low Theory

To quote McKenzie Wark[158], this is the best definition or explanation that I have come across:

I am interested in low theory, which comprise those somewhat rarer moments when, coming out of everyday life, you get a certain milieu that can think itself. It happens when there is a mixing of the classes (another thing higher education doesn't do). It happens in certain spaces that we used to call Bohemia. Low theory is the attempt to think everyday life within practices created in and of and for everyday life, using or misusing high theory to other ends. It happens in collaborative practices that invent their own economies of knowledge.

So, most of this text, where not specifically technological is 'low theory', a non-academic assault on the status quo that has *some* linkages to academic thought or, an academic *style* of thought.

However, as the introduction, there is no overarching, unifying theme, just a series of commentaries. In general, and see (for example) Isiah Berlin[159], *I fear frameworks*.

I'm obliged to think about what I value, as I get older and there are these (at least) in the centre, cooperation, federation, subsidiarity and negotiation. They need each other too. As such, I'm interested in methods, including technical aids and methods of arriving at agreement or compromise.

---

158 https://en.wikipedia.org/wiki/McKenzie_Wark
159 https://plato.stanford.edu/entries/liberty-positive-negative/#TwoConLib

The Algorithmic Anarchist   Hugh Barnard 24/10/21

Loyalty Cards

Throw away all your loyalty cards too, the exchange you are making in return for your privacy and data is a bad bargain. When enough people give up their loyalty cards, a few (minor) things may change, but also, it's a modest rehearsal for the more radical. And, yes, I do not have a single loyalty card, I do have a Co-op card.

Machine Intelligence

Quick read, so, in the main, it isn't. Have a look at the entry for **Artificial Intelligence**, I've grouped machine intelligence with this, following the schema used by Wikipedia.

Mercenaries

It's not noticeable on the surface but more and more conflicts are being partially fought by mercenaries[160]. Weapons of war have always been a huge part of 'trade' (or, for most of us, negative externality) but now the manpower to go with it is being financialised too.

How does this change things? Well, smaller actors, if they are financially powerful can start or intervene in a war, the doctrine of 'small wars[161]', ever present but increasing in the conflict mix. Lack of ideology as a component of conflict, increasing focus on profit.

---

[160] https://www.trtworld.com/americas/six-things-you-should-know-about-modern-mercenaries-of-war-20831
[161] https://www.rand.org/blog/2019/12/bad-idea-assuming-the-small-wars-era-is-over.html

The Algorithmic Anarchist   Hugh Barnard 24/10/21

Resistance to any supra-national intervention or moderation, they are not participants in Geneva Convention (although, this is true of some national combatants now too) and therefore will attack UN, police forces, medical third parties and other non-combatants. So war becomes more unrestrained and more deadly for anyone whatsoever in the war zone. It's evident that all war is bad, this is a new horizon of death, cruelty and danger.

Meta

I have had an idea for a t-shirt that I must get done, sooner or later saying 'Meta is Better' or maybe 'Meta is Betta' I can't decide.

Here is the Urban Dictionary[162] definition, *Meta means about the thing itself. It's seeing the thing from a higher perspective instead of from within the thing, like being self-aware.* So metadata is data *about* a set of data, for example, what is included and how often it's updated.

That example introduces signals analysis, for example making possible deductions from the amount and frequency of exchanges, without being able to read the exchanges themselves. Gordon Welchman[163] pioneered traffic analysis[164], a meta data approach. Incidentally, he was airbrushed from The Imitation Game.

Be Meta!

---

162 https://www.urbandictionary.com/
163 https://en.wikipedia.org/wiki/Gordon_Welchman
164 https://en.wikipedia.org/wiki/Traffic_analysis

The Algorithmic Anarchist   Hugh Barnard 24/10/21

Mischief

I am old enough to remember Ken Kesey's Merry Pranksters[165] and their bus. One of the things the status-quo hates is being laughed at. They can deal more easily with being hated, that's a kind of validation for anyone or anything. However, laughing is a different kind of freedom.

A quote from Steppenwolf[165] "In eternity there is no time, only an instant long enough for a joke." and (probably) from Emma Goldman, "If I can't dance, I don't want to be part of your revolution".

So, personally, I'm not interested in the miserable, normative (silly prole, do this, 'we' know what's best for you) social justice warrior method for evolution. It's authoritarian, apart from being unattractive.

On a more serious note, jokes are memorable memes and part of a radical narrative too, this is a Banksy quote on a wall, just by the entrance to the Blackwall Tunnel: "The lifestyle you have ordered is currently out of stock".

---

165 https://en.wikipedia.org/wiki/Steppenwolf_(novel)

Models

Models[166] appear in modern discourse, notably about Climate Change. The believers say "look at the models, it's really bad" and the denier "it's only a model"[167]. I'm a deep green, so I'm a believer, however both camps are correct. Models are not reality (whatever that is), they are thinner cruder versions of it.

However, this cuts both ways, if the climate models are correct, then ignoring them is catastrophic, if we are 'not sure' (correct to some extent, for example) then we need to apply the precautionary principle[168] to our policies.

Also, overlooked, many of the policies that support climate mitigation and adaptation also lead to a more pleasant, greener, less polluted, healthier world. There are potent arguments that we should adopt some of these policies and directions 'anyway'. This is why, for me, the older Utopias of vast automated factories producing unlimited consumer goods[169] (slightly unfair for the reference, but we're nearly there anyway, as regards plastic toys, for example) are a step in the wrong direction.

To some extent, climate, pollution are now going to limit our choices, but the subset on offer is a pleasant set of choices (see **The Municipal Green Opportunity**, later in book), just not what is sold to us, that's all.

---

166 https://en.wikipedia.org/wiki/Model
167 https://en.wikipedia.org/wiki/All_models_are_wrong (All models are wrong but some are useful)
168 https://en.wikipedia.org/wiki/Precautionary_principle
169 https://en.wikipedia.org/wiki/Fully_Automated_Luxury_Communism

The Algorithmic Anarchist   Hugh Barnard 24/10/21

There's actually a deeper set of points here, concerning causation. If 'correlation is not causation[170]', so what is it? My view is that causal connections can often be expressed via models, though the richness and veracity of the model will vary. Happily, this is also the view of someone a great deal more learned than myself see The Book of Why[171].

I'm a sceptic philosophically so I don't believe we have direct access or insight to the thing itself (world, universe etc. etc.) or the connections between the things. But we often have pretty good models that are useful by being predictive and solution bearing.

Mitigation

Here's the dictionary definition of this, it is '*the action of reducing the severity, seriousness, or painfulness of something*'. The current, contemporary usage is mainly applied to climate change, but there's one or two other applications that are worth examining.

We can perhaps *mitigate* the results of climate change on society, by taking our cars, TVs and consumer goods and going to live underground like mushrooms. OK, that's a caricature to make the point.

We *mitigate* the effects of homelessness on the homeless by providing food banks, soup kitchens and shelters.

---

170 https://en.wikipedia.org/wiki/Correlation_does_not_imply_causation
171 http://bayes.cs.ucla.edu/WHY/

The Algorithmic Anarchist   Hugh Barnard 24/10/21

We *mitigate* market failure by 'volunteering', sometimes, indeed, providing unpaid labour to prop up a decaying state.

These actions are not 'bad', but they support a toxic status quo that refuses to face any of these challenges or decides that 'since I am not affected', there is nothing radical to be done. Mitigating is not evil, but needs to be a precursor to *solving*. I doubt that that proposition will work for climate change for anyone, in fact.

So it's important to be aware and be realistic about any proposal for *mitigating* anything.

Money

This will probably grow into a big entry, in future editions, since it's one of my main areas of concern. The current financial system gives us an unequal, unsustainable, and destructive framework. The associated problem is (some of) the rights of profit-making corporations, especially banks and their fictional role as 'personne morale', a sort-of pretend person. Madison and Jefferson already say huge problems with large scale 'banking' too[172].

I do not believe that corporations and profit are necessarily and logically bad. However, scale plays a significant part, small is *still beautiful*[173].

---

172 https://truthout.org/articles/unequal-protection-jefferson-versus-the-corporate-aristocracy/
173 https://en.wikipedia.org/wiki/Small_Is_Beautiful

The Algorithmic Anarchist   Hugh Barnard 24/10/21

At present, there are many proposals and technologies (the so-called Fintech[174] industry) for new ways of 'doing money'. Some of these can probably be adapted for use in parallel structures.

For one thing, money is technology, from the scratching of symbols on bits of pot to count amounts of grain up to computing, that hasn't changed. The classical definition is here[175], medium of exchange, store of value, measure of value. Without starting a book-length side-issue on value and value theory, this is one bit that is certainly 'wrong', one gun does not equal a large quantity of butter, for example.

We can come back to this, especially as no-one much has figured it out. Meanwhile, look at Theory of Value[176] and more broadly/philosophically Axiology.

On a more practical level, issuance. Currently either government or (worse) private banks can bring money into existence, magically[177]. When money is issued by private institutions, that is via compound interest-bearing debt, *one of the profound bits of wrongness*.

Essentially, when you buy a house, the bank creates (previously) non-existent money (without doing any useful 'work' in the old Marxist sense) and lends it to you. However, if you fail to pay back this fiction, it can then steal something 'real' from you.

This is a good book treating some of the issuance alternatives[178].

---
174 https://en.wikipedia.org/wiki/Financial_technology
175 https://en.wikipedia.org/wiki/Money
176 https://plato.stanford.edu/entries/value-theory/
177 https://en.wikipedia.org/wiki/Money_creation
178 https://www.versobooks.com/books/2706-the-production-of-money

Now for the hopeful bit. We can invent and issue our own money. Either a a complementary (additional) system[179] to the national currency or as a complete alternative, alternative currency.

This or these currencies can take many forms, physical notes and coins, physical ledgers, electronic or scratches on pieces of pottery. The problem is not there, it's more finding the goods and services that will be exchanged and some minimum standards of governance to go with the new creation.

Bitcoin (and Ethereum, Tether etc. etc.) is, of course, an example and (if you will) a proof of this. Trouble is, it is already recuperated and (even if not) doesn't help us towards any desirable future. More probably a tech-liberatarian dystopia in the worse case.

Music

Apart from 'having the power to soothe savage breasts' (one presumes that there are people attached to them), it's good in so many other ways too.

But don't just listen, *make some*. My generation learnt the guitar (tons of free and paid lessons on YouTube), easy to start and lots of songs take a week or so to learn. Traditionally, protest songs too, make your own up and publish them, there's a long tradition in folk music.

---

179 http://www.asocam.org/sites/default/files/publicaciones/files/0e88efe418781c74da1a053b55f0af5f.pdf

The Algorithmic Anarchist   Hugh Barnard 24/10/21

Making music isn't consumption, it's an activity that is nearly free, once you have an instrument. I think that my first guitar in about 1965 was about £5, from the much regretted shop, near my mother's hardware shop in Hornchurch. I've had one ever since.

And a last idea in this subject, it's good for mental health as well, like running.

Narrative

Narrative (as John Lanchester[180] said) has moved out of literature into politics, where, in the mainstream and on social media, it has mutated malignantly into post-truth story telling and spin. This, for example, is one more reason to leave Facebook[181], or, if you really, really must stay, ignore all 'News' except maybe the most stupid stuff.

However, I believe that there are (at least) three nouns that are worth providing counter narratives for. They are commercialisation (especially financialisation), competition and scarcity.

Commercialisation and financialisation are the modern forms of clearance[182] and enclosure[183], eating into ideas of general accessibility (obvious examples being housing and healthcare) and the remains of the commons[184], for example, public libraries and green space.

---
180 https://en.wikipedia.org/wiki/John_Lanchester
181 #DeleteFacebook on Twitter, you know you want to.
182 https://en.wikipedia.org/wiki/Highland_Clearances
183 https://en.wikipedia.org/wiki/Enclosure
184 https://en.wikipedia.org/wiki/Commons

The Algorithmic Anarchist   Hugh Barnard 24/10/21

Somehow, everything will be so much 'better', if the 'true' monetary value is explicit for every service and facility, see **Fair Value**. My favourite book about this, mainly about justice, is 'What Money Cannot Buy[185]'. Read it.

Competition is discussed elsewhere, but appears in every prize, grant application, job application and piece of entertainment (X Factor, cooking competitions etc.). Always judged and commented by experts[186] who are somehow better than us. Of course, if one did not compete in the vain hope of attention from our (mainstream media selected) superiors, *we could cooperate*. Our cake might not be as pretty, but it would be ours.

Scarcity is a societal means of control linked to financialisation. If 'money' is scarce (remember 'money's too tight to mention'[187]?) then control is maximal. Debt[188] and inflation helps this story along too. We need to distinguish between money being scarce and 'stuff' being scarce. I'd argue that the locally organised foodbanks, whilst being a scandal, are also a step in the right direction. Better still that we help neighbours in difficulty directly and acknowledge that our government and administrations are either corrupt or incompetent or both.

---

185 https://scholar.harvard.edu/sandel/publications/what-money-cant-buy-moral-limits-markets
186 https://plato.stanford.edu/entries/foucault/
187 https://youtu.be/DrUB0g8Vjgg
188 https://en.wikipedia.org/wiki/Debt:_The_First_5000_Years

The Algorithmic Anarchist   Hugh Barnard 24/10/21

Open Everything

This sounds like 'old hippie' stuff doesn't it? Let's hear the stoned, whiny "Everything should be free, man", or the more modern "Everything should be free, person" does not have the same ring either. Joke over, if it was.

However, knowledge and computer code, for example, are non-rivalrous[189], if you know A, that doesn't mean it's been used up and I cannot know A. If I use a program B, that will not prevent you from using a copy. I'd argue (at some later time) that knowledge is usually anti-rivalrous, the more people become knowledgeable, the more wider society benefits. Same, as Hollywood knows, for digital versions of films and series.

Obviously here, there are some things to be worked out. Production of modern knowledge (I'm thinking of drugs research followed by the production of useful drugs) is far from zero-cost but the price point and ownership are sub-optimal for society, the world and especially the developing world.

Second different example, academic journals and apparently students e-books[190], same thing non-zero production price but price at consumption point that we can confidently call 'gouging'. This means that 'poorer' knowledge consumers who are capable of doing something constructive with it are excluded. Knowledge for the rich and connected, like the Middle Ages.

---

189 https://en.wikipedia.org/wiki/Rivalry_(economics)
190 https://www.theguardian.com/education/2021/jan/29/price-gouging-from-covid-student-ebooks-costing-up-to-500-more-than-in-print

The constructive act could just be 'learning' too, in the sense of life enrichment. It's often fun to know new stuff.

The journals and software are a common goods riddle (Common Pool Resources[191], taking the language of the entirely admirable Elinor Ostrom[192]) with suppliers, consumers and infrastructure but they are not 'used up' with increasing numbers of users.

I believe that coops and mutualist structures are part of the answer to both of these, they do not make everything 'free', but they do align prices with costs, rather than profit maximisation and rentier[193]-style shareholder 'dividend'.

Open Source

There's some controversy about this, since the Free Software Movement[194] founded by Stallman preceded and co-exists with this software appellation. Open source concentrates more on use and licence, whereas the Free Software Movement concentrates on all those and ethics of development and usage.

Thus there's now a hybrid appellation FOSS, Free and Open Source Software. There are also a number of models that enable organisations to make money without closing the software.

Even within the stricter Free Software about payment, the two ideas of *free as in beer* and *free as in speech* are untangled.

---

191 https://www.thecommonsjournal.org/articles/10.18352/ijc.305/
192 https://en.wikipedia.org/wiki/Elinor_Ostrom
193 https://en.wikipedia.org/wiki/Rentier_capitalism
194 https://en.wikipedia.org/wiki/Free_software_movement

The Algorithmic Anarchist   Hugh Barnard 24/10/21

Since it's apparently another hippie-dippie thing, who uses it? Well, nearly everyone from investment banks to governments. Indeed, some governments have started to stipulate use.

Probably the most famous unknown piece of software, used is Apache[195], a web server that is used by about 34% of domains at a recent count[196]. Nginx[197] (engine x), also (free version) open source is a similar size chunk too. There's actually a commercial free-riding problem with all this, in that open source developers code and then (many) commercial organisations use, without giving anything back.

Parallel Structures

Of course, the Maoists in Nepal[198] are a good example of 'how far' parallel structures can go. My own views are towards the lower parts of of the Maslow triangle with a view to partial autonomy and partial self-sufficiency. More of a *turning away* and *turning back on* than an *overthrowing*.

It's worth noting that if no-one whatsoever shopped at ASDA, it would close[199] (but see the entry for **Brands** and **Crash on Consumption**). In the same way, if the parallel structures increase in strength, then one can expect/hope some of the existing structures to wither away.

_____

195 https://httpd.apache.org/
196 https://news.netcraft.com/archives/2018/01/19/january-2018-web-server-survey.html
197 https://en.wikipedia.org/wiki/Nginx
198 https://www.jstor.org/stable/4418464 (preview only, as it's *jstor*)
199 Qu'il suffirait que les gens ne les achètent plus pour que ça se vende pas! (Coluche)

For a number of reasons (we need it, I'm a great admirer of Winstanley and the Diggers[200]) I tend to concentrate on food and energy. Housing is a harder problem to solve immediately, too.

People's AI

There are now a great many open source tools[201] for machine learning and other forms of sub-symbolic AI.

It's up to us to use these for our general benefit and, in turn, open source the investigations and results. This approach, of course, meshes with **Citizen Science**, open knowledge[202] and open access publishing[203].

Port-80

As any fule know[204], this was the original port for serving web content. Since non-encrypted passwords and transited via port-80, encrypted web traffic has now moved to port-443, the home of https[205] (the padlock thing, see **Public Key Cryptography**).

---

200 https://en.wikipedia.org/wiki/Diggers
201 https://www.airesources.org/
202 https://okfn.org/ (Open Knowledge Foundation)
203 https://www.jisc.ac.uk/guides/an-introduction-to-open-access
204 https://en.wikipedia.org/wiki/Nigel_Molesworth
205 https://en.wikipedia.org/wiki/HTTPS

However, stepping back, the web, originally disorganised, fun and hyperlinked has now become 'sites', Twitter, Facebook, Tumblr etc., a series of walled gardens[206] owned by vectorialists[207]. Spied on by 'everyone', full of advertising, malware, subtle misinformation campaigns and astroturfing, incitements to gamble and buy stuff, it is not a space or welcoming structure for anything radical now.

My first 'modest proposal[208]' is to move to some other non 80, non 443 port or work out some spectrum-hopping/port-hopping scheme and establish a new people's cyberspace there. Of course, some junk would filter in, but then we could move it again, causing a great deal of corporate pain and anguish in the process. Or we could just 'threaten' to move again.

However there's a great many other ways to do this, currently, for example, something based on the Gemini protocol[209], may work out or Freenet[210] may become more visible and greatly adopted.

Port-443

The padlocky port. In principle all web communication via this port is encrypted. However, this is by convention only, there can be encrypted or non-encrypted web communication on any port that is not used for anything else.

See also Gemini protocol, above.

---
206 https://medium.com/mediarithmics-what-is/what-is-a-walled-garden-and-why-it-is-the-strategy-of-google-facebook-and-amazon-ads-platform-296ddeb784b1
207 https://en.wikipedia.org/wiki/A_Hacker_Manifesto
208 https://www.gutenberg.org/files/1080/1080-h/1080-h.htm
209 https://en.wikipedia.org/wiki/Gemini_(protocol)
210 https://en.wikipedia.org/wiki/Freenet

The Algorithmic Anarchist   Hugh Barnard 24/10/21

Printed Supplements

You may have noticed that newspapers and magazines have additional printed material, usually publicity folded into them.

However, *you can add your own material to these*, especially if they are on some kind of stand. The same applies to folded promotional brochures of the kind that are often found in shopping centres. This is especially useful, if you have some specific commentary to make that is related to the original printed material. Enough said.

Public Key Cryptography

Best way to explain this, *it is very probably your friend*. Until recently the USA banned the export of this kind of cryptography[211], having decided that it was a weapon.

There are two bits, a public key that you publish and a private bit that you keep to yourself. You can have the public bit printed on a card as a QR code[212], for example. People can then encode messages that only the holder of the private bit can decode.

There's a lot more than that, but specifically see 'web of trust[213]' and 'key signing parties[214]' decentralised methods of putting a little extra confidence into the keys that are being exchanged.

---

211 https://www.schneier.com/books/applied-cryptography/ (book)
212 https://en.wikipedia.org/wiki/QR_code
213 https://en.wikipedia.org/wiki/Web_of_trust
214 https://en.wikipedia.org/wiki/Key_signing_party

The Algorithmic Anarchist   Hugh Barnard 24/10/21

Récupération[215]

This is another useful concept from the Situationists[216]. Simply, if something, a subversive idea, a subversive concept appears to be surfacing and gaining traction, it is sugar coated and absorbed into the mainstream, where it can be appropriated and transformed into something neutral and (perhaps) profitable.

Actually, hipsters and 'hipsterism' (if there is such a word) are a major example of this effect. They have adopted eccentricity as a fashion statement but are not eccentric. In fact, given their clear obsession with Apple products (what is a person with an iPhone, an iPad and an iPod, answer an iDiot, not funny, but it's made me slightly calmer) they are consumers.

On the subject of art too, if it is too challenging, it can be bought and hidden away or used in another context. A current example, Hendrix's version of All Along the Watchtower has apparently been licensed to Chanel. Previously (and worsely, to coin a word) Ezy Rider was licensed to Barclays Bank, one of the most hateful banks on the planet Earth.

Of course 'money doesn't talk, it swears[217]'.

---

215 https://en.wikipedia.org/wiki/Recuperation_(politics)
216 https://www.cddc.vt.edu/sionline/ (Situationist archive)
217 https://en.wikipedia.org/wiki/It%27s_Alright,_Ma_(I%27m_Only_Bleeding)

The Algorithmic Anarchist   Hugh Barnard 24/10/21

Scarcity

One of the fundamental, together with money (and therefore 'austerity'), levers of control for modern society. I'm really, really, really sorry but we'd like to X (because we are decent people) but there's not enough for everybody. Please compete and disagree with each other, it's nature's way[218].

To take the easiest scarcity subject first, money, the current arrangements (majority private issuance as interest bearing[219]) will inevitably lead to scarcity and inequality. I do not believe that this was originally a conspiracy, because money was an iterative creation, but the status quo is maintained *by those who benefit from it*. In this case, especially those who create and handle the current form of money, the banks and associated. There are also some huge problems of governance and democracy associated with this, since these private institutions are a major influence on the well being of all who happen to use that currency.

There are (at least) three alternatives, a) elected government controls issuance, not the case at the moment, since, for example, the Bank of England is (somewhat) independent b) multiple smaller currencies with non-bank issuance c) mixture of a) and b) for example. Finally, keep status quo except that the banks have much tighter issuance parameters and some banks are downsized. The multiple smaller currencies movement is growing somewhat with the Bristol, Brixton and Lewes pound, for example. However, most of these currencies are backed by the national currency and are therefore not independent in any meaningful way.

---

218 Oh no it isn't!
219 https://positivemoney.org/how-money-%20works/how-banks-%20create-money/

The Algorithmic Anarchist   Hugh Barnard 24/10/21

Search-engine

Well, you know, Google. As in, let me Google that for you etc. etc. But however, quick convenient and efficient it may be, it is a vector for consumerism (for example, stuff to buy will come out at the top) and the status quo (radical results may be 'hidden', although recent research has Google currently as left-centre leaning for results) and, of course, paid advertising is a dominant feature. Also, it will track you.

This is something of a problem, since technically it is the 'best' one. However, for example DuckDuckGo[220] is coming up and you can help it be 'better'. So each search that you switch from Google to DuckDuckGo is a finger in the eye for Googlezon/Facebook. Note this is ordinal, DuckDuckGo has its problems but still better than Google. Try Ecosia[221], if you'd like some trees planted.

Better still, build your own[222] for your local area or for a specific specialised subdomain, ask for donations for the bandwidth or allow only local/ethical business advertising. All the major search engines have a malware problem, so there's space for something more specialised and focused.

I've given a couple of talks[223] on building search engines, together with some of the more obvious technical and ethical challenges.

---

220 https://duckduckgo.com/
221 https://info.ecosia.org/?tt=fa7e1292
222 https://www.pearson.com/uk/educators/higher-education-educators/program/Baeza-Yates-Modern-Information-Retrieval/PGM407074.html (technical book)
223 https://hughbarnard.org/index.php/2021/10/23/search-engine-talk/

Security Tools

These include Tor[224], Tails[225] and, in fact Linux. But if you're that worried, it's better simply to stay off-line and off-mobile-phone with what-it-is, that you're worrying about. Tor, in principle will provide anonymous browsing, but, there are rumours that one of the US security services has broken into it.

Tails is a secure operating system based on Linux, usually delivered on a CD or USB, so that you can use a machine without leaving a trace of your usage.

From 2106, in the UK you may also want a VPN[226] (Virtual Private Network) connection. It *may* (if the supplier is honest and competent) deny your browsing history, for example from the organisations[227] that now have potential access to it. Since, anyway, we are dealing with the Civil Service and the UK police, this information will leaked and misused routinely, apart from the so-called 'legitimate' uses. There is no guarantee, of course, that the VPN supplier itself is secure (many of them say that they do not keep any logs, a good start, but how to check) and many of them are USA corporations and therefore subject to US not UK law. Proton is subject to Swiss Law and has acceded to at least one request from the French authorities[228].

---

224 https://www.torproject.org/download/
225 https://tails.boum.org/
226 https://en.wikipedia.org/wiki/Virtual_private_network
227 https://www.legislation.gov.uk/ukpga/2000/23/schedule/1
228 https://techcrunch.com/2021/09/06/protonmail-logged-ip-address-of-french-activist-after-order-by-swiss-authorities/

Linux itself is almost certainly 'better' than Windows in this respect. Because it's open source, in principle you can build it from scratch after inspecting every line of code in the build (but as Ken Thompson pointed out in 1984, one would need to trust the compiler[229], as well). Also, Windows viruses will be ineffective, though there are other attacks directed at Linux.

Smart Meters

In the UK, at least, there's been a decade long push towards Smart Meters[230], expensive television advertising and associated social media PR. There are (at least) two layers of criticism, technical and societal.

First the technical, the current UK set are based on the SMETS1[231] standard which is being superseded by SMETS2[232], first roll-out available in 2018. The older ones are apparently being 'upgraded' to full functionality, sometime real soon. For example, some of the older ones wouldn't tolerate a change of supplier. None of them in the UK, as far as I'm aware have a P1 port[233] so that data can be modelled in house. This is the case in the Netherlands, for example.

Next societal, user data access (see above), security, use of data for marketing, and remote disconnection are some of the areas of concern.

---

229 https://wiki.c2.com/?TheKenThompsonHack
230 https://en.wikipedia.org/wiki/Smart_meter
231 https://www.smartme.co.uk/technical.html
232 see 155
233 https://xebia.com/blog/how-to-read-gas-and-electricity-measurements-from-your-smart-meter/

The Algorithmic Anarchist   Hugh Barnard 24/10/21

First, it is not currently possible to easily access a usage data stream within the dwelling, output is limited to an idiot (in home display) display with figures and (sometimes) smiley faces. So, any significant data logging is pretty much hidden from the consumer, or massaged into something meaningless. As far as genuine, focused household level green initiatives are concerned, this is near useless.

Security, in spite of all the waffle about keys, DCC etc., it is probable that either Zigbee[234] or SMS messages can be hacked. Everything is, sooner rather than later. This may provide meta-data on occupancy *or not* of the dwelling which therefore may not need the contents of messages, just frequency, for example.

The data itself, seems to be firmly in the hands of the suppliers and (no doubt) the government who can use it, to game the energy market, craft consumer marketing information, surge pricing[235] (I'm not against this, done for practical rather than for-profit reasons), eavesdropping and the list goes one. Whilst I don't believe in a conspiracy, there is a principal agent problem[236] and a non-alignment of interests here that makes me nervous.

Finally, remote disconnection, both government and supplier have denied that they will do this, but the capability is there. It's a good way of sanctioning squatters, difficult customers, dissidents and other, *without any of the legal difficulties of physical entry to a property*. Even, as a threat, it's a pretty decent tool.

No-one much wanted them in France, so they had to legislate.

---

234 https://zigbeealliance.org/solution/zigbee/
235 https://en.wikipedia.org/wiki/Dynamic_pricing
236 https://en.wikipedia.org/wiki/Principal–agent_problem

The Algorithmic Anarchist   Hugh Barnard 24/10/21

Spectacle

For those of you who are not familiar with Guy Debord[237] (and the Situationists) who wrote the Society of the Spectacle[238], try a little light(er) reading about it[239]. Indeed, it's pretty heavy going. There's a pretty good entry in Wikipedia under Spectacle (critical theory)[240].

Two main take-aways (these are mine, incidentally) a) commodities now rule us b) we have become more and more passive in the face of this. My 'extended' take-away, is that *nothing, except maybe some spreadsheets and computer programs*, is in charge now, just numbers and indexes. Algorithmic nihilism. We are alienated in the Marxist sense and ache to live, but numbers will not let us. *We need to start to throw away these numbers.*

This insight now needs some re-working and extension to deal more thoroughly with the digital, social media and 'device' (especially the smartphone) world. For example, a great deal of our interpersonal relations are now mediated (or we allow to be mediated) by what McKenzie Wark calls the vectorialists (see the entry for **Vectorialists** too).

Finally, and I thank someone in the Anarchist Book Fair for this information, J. B. Priesley invented the word 'Admass[241]' in about 1955, that conveys something of the same, a world dominated by manufactured and manipulated desire.

---

237 https://en.wikipedia.org/wiki/Guy_Debord
238 https://en.wikipedia.org/wiki/The_Society_of_the_Spectacle
239 https://hyperallergic.com/313435/an-illustrated-guide-to-guy-debords-the-society-of-the-spectacle/
240 https://en.wikipedia.org/wiki/Spectacle_(critical_theory)
241 https://en.wiktionary.org/wiki/admass

Also, it's fair to say, that this is one of the main motors of this text, the idea that we can break away from corporate and for-profit owned platforms towards platform cooperatives and non-profit local digital islands. These might reflect our world in a different, co-operative, non-competitive way too.

Speed

Here, as usual, I hark back to Energy and Equity[242], just riffling through, to write this, I find 'people move quite well on their feet'. Yes, indeed. So why don't we do more of that? My belief is that late-stage capitalism has captured the rhythm of our lives and demands that we be 'fast', 'efficient' and 'productive'. This last, 'productive' is a word that we hear incessantly from governments as to why we cannot be paid more.

Consider, under some new order, we slow down and only make five plastic dolls per day, disaster, sales and profits are down, the shareholders become angry. Profits must increase every year, since dividends, the share price and directors remuneration must increase, so, everything must go faster. Of course, in this simple activity, industrial robots could do everything and the 'product' is a pure pollutant, so no need to rush.

---

242 http://debate.uvm.edu/asnider/Ivan_Illich/Ivan%20Illich_Energy%20and%20Equity.pdf (the book as a pdf)

The Algorithmic Anarchist   Hugh Barnard 24/10/21

But speed is a certainly a form of power relationship, our bosses tell us to hurry up, we have (arbitrary, often) 'deadlines' to create unnecessary and unhealthy pressure in our lives. We rush from home to work, we get into our cars to rush to distant shopping centres, to buy things that we don't need. Life in the West is culturally fast, but this speed is contingent and can be unravelled in many cases.

Price and access to speed has distorted urban geography too, since we are car bound, we can put everything into malls and out of town boxes, shuttling backwards and forwards, ignoring the potential sociability of our decaying town centres. OK, that's not the only factor, but it's a major one.

I agree that when lives are in danger or suffering, we need to move fast, for the rest we can take our time.

Sponsorship

To head a little in the direction of Ambrose Bierce[243] (The Devil's Dictionary[244]), 'sponsorship is a way for corporate world to shoehorn its way into places that it does not belong by simply spending money'.

I've gave up running my favourite half-marathon for a while (yes, I'm getting old, as well) because it was sponsored by Virgin Health an organisation that has sued the NHS because it didn't like the result of a contract attribution.

---

243 https://en.wikipedia.org/wiki/Ambrose_Bierce
244 https://en.wikipedia.org/wiki/The_Devil%27s_Dictionary

The Algorithmic Anarchist   Hugh Barnard 24/10/21

I'm looking forward to the day when some of the supposedly socialist fiefdoms, London mayor, Hackney, Newham actually roll with their principles and kick these people out.

It's also notable that, at time of writing (2019), Active Newham cooperates with ParkLives behind which is the Coca-Cola company, a particularly perverse decision. Actually, updated, they've decided to stop, well done.

Street Art

I meant, this year, to write an essay for a (now defunct) website called 'Art and Anger'. However a smaller meditation here will have to do.

At the start and sporadically through the 20th century some art was also associated with political activism and/or political activists. The ranges from Dadaism[245] (which could be argued as being absurdist or maybe nihilist, but fun) to Guernica[246] and through to Banksy now. Banksy is good example of Debordian 'recuperation', something that was subversive is re-absorbed, given a price, made the subject of consumer fetishism etc. etc. Any edge is immediately blunted.

Currently there is a) tagging b) scribbling c) pieces of fairly narcissistic and samey mural, no doubt, often, here in London, with the same originators.

_____

245 https://en.wikipedia.org/wiki/Dada
246 https://en.wikipedia.org/wiki/Guernica_(Picasso)

However, the walls, the streets, important elsewhere[247] (I'm writing this in the UK) are a greatly undervalued resource for the expression of anger, change, mockery, and mischief. For example, as part of my people-networked project, supposing that the same thing (a philosopher would say many tokens of the same thing) appeared in many, many places at once. That's quite an important and striking counter narrative, immediately.

How to communicate any consistent message faithfully, given revisionists and class traitors (I'm joking, I think it is time to discard certain ancient Marxist tropes) within the communicators? This is part of an interesting class of problems called the Byzantine Generals[248] problem.

For myself, I have been thinking about a project using only Linear B, discussed earlier, but it's syllabic. Shavian Noto is alphabetic though[249]. See the entry on **Mischief**, too.

---

247 https://www.google.com/search?q=street+art+north+africa
248 https://www.microsoft.com/en-us/research/uploads/prod/2016/12/The-Byzantine-Generals-Problem.pdf
249 https://fonts.google.com/noto/specimen/Noto+Sans+Shavian

Subsidiarity[250]

The principle of deciding and acting at the lowest level possible. If it can be done street by street, better that it be done so. Village by village, same thing. This does not necessarily imply flattened hierarchies, in fact, it may imply Bookchin[251] like multiple level assemblies that feed into each other. This is the method used by the Kurds[252], and described by Carne Ross[253] in the Accidental Anarchist[254] (qv).

OK, this makes for a more complex system, but also for a much more representative one. People own the decisions, even the bad ones, of which there will surely be a few. Actually, it's baked into the EU but they ignore it for something more centralised whenever possible.

---

250 https://en.wikipedia.org/wiki/Subsidiarity
251 https://en.wikipedia.org/wiki/Murray_Bookchin
252 https://en.wikipedia.org/wiki/Kurds
253 https://en.wikipedia.org/wiki/Carne_Ross
254 https://www.youtube.com/watch?v=Zh-RQG0xYAM

The Algorithmic Anarchist   Hugh Barnard 24/10/21

System[255], The

What exactly do I mean by system, apart from the whiny hippy 'system' and 'the man'? First a little tour, I'm an admirer of the Situationists and therefore the system (for me) is whatever underlies the Spectacle. I'm not a big believer in the rule of the Lizards[256] or Bilderbergers[257], however, I agree with Susan George[258] (qv) that, if a group of people have an agenda that converges, there needn't be 'explicit' conspiracy.

So I'm talking (mainly), neoclassical economics[259] and its *spectacular*[260] narrative (hard work will lead to success, competition is always beneficial, the market is efficient, scarcity is universal and natural, the poor are feckless etc.), the current way of 'doing' money and the reification of markets, for example 'the market hopes', 'the market fears' have made social aspirations subordinate to arithmetic. The wound-up springs (illusory fiduciary duty to maximise[261]) inside corporations and the idea that they are a 'personne morale[262]' and can speak, all of this does a great deal of damage.

_____

255 https://en.wikipedia.org/wiki/Economic_system
256 https://www.theguardian.com/lifeandstyle/2016/apr/07/conspiracy-theory-paranoia-aliens-illuminati-beyonce-vaccines-cliven-bundy-jfk
257 https://en.wikipedia.org/wiki/Bilderberg_meeting
258 https://en.wikipedia.org/wiki/Susan_George_(political_scientist)
259 https://en.wikipedia.org/wiki/Neoclassical_economics
260 Lying
261 https://medium.com/bull-market/there-is-no-effective-fiduciary-duty-to-maximize-profits-939ae50d0572
262 https://fr.wikipedia.org/wiki/Personne_morale

The Algorithmic Anarchist   Hugh Barnard 24/10/21

It's a tangle or as system theorists say, a wicked problem[263]. Ultimately, my own belief is that no-one is in charge, or maybe there's a single spreadsheet somewhere with a list of indicators that must somehow be maximised. We've lost our way.

My route to restoration is essentially non-violent, neo-liberalism has plenty of open interfaces, if we move our bank account, that's an act, if we boycott (even partially, I buy from Amazon but mainly from elsewhere, it's my *last* choice) if we grow vegetables and/or forage, that's an act. If we refuse to consume, or cut down, that's pretty powerful[264][265]. At a richer level if we or (more and more) universities divest with our retirement funds or don't buy things that we don't need, that's an act. *Every act is subject to conscious choice*[266] and an act, co-ordinated and larger campaigns are clearly more effective, one more reason for the technical content in this document.

They

Repeat to yourself, every night, 'there is no they', as in 'they ought', for example, it's 'you'. See also the book, I YOU WE THEM[267] by Dan Gretton

---

263 https://en.wikipedia.org/wiki/Wicked_problem
264 https://www.theguardian.com/environment/2021/oct/20/we-need-to-stop-buying-stuff-and-i-know-just-the-people-to-persuade-us
265 https://holmgren.com.au/wp-content/uploads/2014/01/Crash-on-demand.pdf
266 OK, so this inches towards this: *Act only according to that maxim whereby you can at the same time will that it should become a universal law.*
267 https://www.penguin.co.uk/books/110/1107904/i-you-we-them/9780099592372.html

The Algorithmic Anarchist   Hugh Barnard 24/10/21

Think Tanks

Not always a bad thing, if we understand who is funding them. However there is currently a cluster, mainly in Tufton Street and Lord North Street that are mysteriously funded and connection to the Atlas Network[268] slogan 'strengthening the worldwide freedom network'. In this case, this means freedom from any government regulation, safety, competition, ecology and all the other things that keep up safe.

These particular 'think tanks', a better word is lobbyists have connections to right wing think tanks in the USA[269], via the Atlas network. They are also, probably, partially funded by right wing, climate change deniers who make money from fossil fuels, one of the activities they with to be 'free' to continue with. Finally, there are direct connections[270] into the current UK Conservative party, including some documented donations.

Trolling

I see some forms of trolling[271] as a public service. For example, I spend (waste, some would say) a certain amount of my week trolling right wing 'think tanks' (lobbyists from the so-called Atlas Network[272]) and commentators. I don't insult or name call, but I do draw attention to some of their other activities (cash for access, guns) and affiliations.

---
268 https://www.atlasnetwork.org/
269 https://www.theguardian.com/politics/2019/nov/29/rightwing-thinktank-conservative-boris-johnson-brexit-atlas-network
270 https://www.theguardian.com/politics/2019/nov/29/rightwing-thinktank-conservative-boris-johnson-brexit-atlas-network
271 https://en.wikipedia.org/wiki/Internet_troll
272 https://www.atlasnetwork.org/ (so nasty that it has two footnotes!)

The Algorithmic Anarchist   Hugh Barnard 24/10/21

On these think tanks, there is really just one, but it is a hydra with many heads in 'conversation' thus creating the impression of something more substantial.

I do most of my trolling on Twitter where I am @hughbarnard since I am a transparency maximalist, I have deleted myself from LinkedIn and Facebook and advise others to do the same.

Vectorialist[273]

This is McKenzie Wark[274]'s word, not my own. The modern, skewed version of those that 'own the means of production' in the sense of those that own and control the digital exchanges. That would therefore be the owners (shareholders) of Facebook, EE (biggest mobile subscriber base in the UK), Amazon, LinkedIn, Microsoft and Google, for example.

Instead of talking to people and even visiting their houses to have a cup of tea, our lives are passing through the hands of these 'owners' who are profiting from each conversation, each *like*, each *poke* and all the emojiis laid end to end in a useless row. All the distractions of games with candy (incidentally there is protein folding game[275], SETI[276] etc. at least this is useful), little things that jump and twitch, all theirs. We are steadily encasing ourselves in ever new forms of societal alienation and (what the existentialists would probably call) inauthenticity.

Don't.

---
273 https://en.wikipedia.org/wiki/A_Hacker_Manifesto
274 https://en.wikipedia.org/wiki/McKenzie_Wark
275 https://en.wikipedia.org/wiki/Foldit
276 https://en.wikipedia.org/wiki/SETI@home (discontinued currently)

The Algorithmic Anarchist   Hugh Barnard 24/10/21

There are (at least) two remedies to this ill. The first, is to start giving up these habits, downgrade your smart phone to a feature phone or give it up altogether (I have a mobile phone, but it spends a great deal of its time in my kitchen drawer) and look at the web etc. only in certain moments of the day. Do not be an phone addict, a slave wandering around, gazing down.

The second is the platform cooperative[277], we keep some of this infrastructure, but maintain and own it 'ourselves' within cooperative or mutual structures. After all, Ivan Illich (read Energy and Equity[278]) praised the telephone as an 'instrument of conviviality' and I, personally, do not believe that Utopia is something very Calvinist[279], horsehair shirts and imposed 'simplicity'.

Via Negativa[280]

From the article 'there is immense power in improvement by subtraction - an idea called *via negativa*'. Apparently, we're not terrifically good at this[281]. Late stage capitalism certainly isn't, because removal and simplification hardly ever offers opportunities for profit.

---

277 https://en.wikipedia.org/wiki/Platform_cooperative
278 http://debate.uvm.edu/asnider/Ivan_Illich/Ivan%20Illich_Energy%20and%20Equity.pdf
279 https://en.wikipedia.org/wiki/Calvinism
280 https://www.wealest.com/articles/via-negativa
281 https://www.nature.com/articles/d41586-021-00592-0

A central example is illness. Illness offers opportunities for medicines, interventions and a huge infrastructure. Well organised and communication public health subtracts some of these *opportunities*. Better for the system to encourage (for example) poor diet and supplements, rather than good diet and no supplements. Supplements mean packaging and manufacturing too, win-win.

Poor air means a market for air purifiers, and on and on (pace Vonnegut). This is also one of the core ideas in Taleb's Antifragile[282].

Volunteering

Also known as slavery. For example, top of the Olympics shit-pile was paid about £450K per year, yet the 'gamesmakers[283]' were conned into volunteering for something that was a complete waste of public money. I hesitate to think how many homes or hospitals wards could have benefited from £12 billion or so, wasted on the Olympics, original budget £3 billion.

Also large NGO[284]s and large 'charities', same thing. To be brutal, we are propping up the current system by letting the government/banks starve people and then using major charities to feed them. Some proponents of accelerationism[285] would probably agree. Local foodbanks and, in general, local solidarity, yes, though, preferably without transiting via the national charities.

---

282 https://en.wikipedia.org/wiki/Antifragile_(book)
283 https://www.olympic.org/news/volunteers-helping-to-make-the-games-happen
284 https://en.wikipedia.org/wiki/Non-governmental_organization
285 https://en.wikipedia.org/wiki/Accelerationism

It is also now true that heads of the larger charities style themselves 'CEO[286]' and pay themselves large salaries. It's becoming a business. I notice that, as I write this, trust in UK charities has reached its lowest point. Also, as I write the RSPCA and the British Heart Foundation are being examined by the ICO for various data offences including financial profiling, to see, presumably, whether there was more to be milked from their donors.

Walled Gardens[287]

This entry should also read 'connecting the walled gardens' or 'closing the gaps'. In the 1980s and 1990s, internet email was not generally available, but we did have Compuserve[288] and AOL[289] (American Online). One of the 'great' things for these providers is that one *could only communicate with a member of the same service*. In modern terms a Gmail user could not communicate with a Hotmail user, for example.

Now, with Facebook especially, we're going in the same direction, Facebook communicates (mainly) with Facebook. Also, like the Hotel California, one cannot conveniently leave[290], since a) the mass of people are on it[291] b) at present there are no alternatives, at that scale. See also **Federation** for ideas about human scale, responsive, community owned alternatives to these monoliths.

---

286 https://en.wikipedia.org/wiki/Chief_executive_officer
287 https://medium.com/mediarithmics-what-is/what-is-a-walled-garden-and-why-it-is-the-strategy-of-google-facebook-and-amazon-ads-platform-296ddeb784b1
288 https://en.wikipedia.org/wiki/CompuServe
289 https://en.wikipedia.org/wiki/AOL
290 https://youtu.be/EqPtz5qN7HM
291 https://en.wikipedia.org/wiki/Reed%27s_law (utility in large social networks)

The Algorithmic Anarchist		Hugh Barnard 24/10/21

Secondly, closing the gaps. When you search for something on Google (that neo-liberal display window and shopping channel, *it's not a search engine*) you will be directed towards Google's preferred 'shops' or Amazon[292]. So the experience is seamless, all your 'needs' will be met by Google, Amazon, Facebook, EBay or Microsoft, no need to look elsewhere. I used to buy used books from Abe Books[293], but Amazon bought it, so now I am reluctant to do so.

Governments could, of course, start to apply anti-trust statutes and instruments but seem reluctant to do so. In the case of the UK, they don't mind if these organisations don't really pay taxes either. Partly this is a problem created by UK tax code though, at time of writing about seventeen thousand pages[294]. So much for Thoreau's 'simplify, simplify[295]'!

What is to be Done?

Что делать[296]? This is a provocation, since it's the title of Lenin's pamphlet and previously the title of Chernyshevsky's novel[297]. However, most modern intellectual life is (conveniently) about analysis and searching for facts, not any kind of 'doing', what political theorists tend to call, pompously, praxis. So I've placed this here as a reminder, as Sartre did not say *to do is to be* but it's a useful thought anyway.

---

[292] https://ec.europa.eu/commission/presscorner/detail/en/IP_21_3143
[293] https://www.abebooks.co.uk/
[294] https://www.theguardian.com/commentisfree/2015/feb/13/britain-tax-code-17000-pages-long-dog-whistle-very-rich
[295] https://simple.wikiquote.org/wiki/Henry_David_Thoreau
[296] https://en.wikipedia.org/wiki/What_Is_to_Be_Done%3F
[297] https://en.wikipedia.org/wiki/What_Is_to_Be_Done%3F_(novel)

The Algorithmic Anarchist   Hugh Barnard 24/10/21

WMD[298]

No, not those. I'm thinking about weapons of mass distraction, the TV, the Web, social media and mainstream press. All of these have a single agenda with slight addition of different flavours, government flavour, consumption flavour, and big business flavour for example.

However the underlying agenda is the preservation of the status quo, things must not change or, if they do, not in any radical or perceptible way. The deckchairs may get moved around a little though. There's always spectator sport in all its forms as an overlay of distraction too.

Written Record

This came up in conversation recently. When complaining or contesting to a large organisation, they will probably want to deal with the matter on the phone ('data', they'll always want your phone number) since that will leave no written record.

Refuse this and only accept an email exchange or printed letters. It's worth noting, as well, that 'contact form' complaints can disappear too. There are two, at least, underlying messages here. First, customer service reduces profits and must be reduced to a minimum. Second, if there is no written trace this increases deniability from the organisation side, hence lost statistics for fault products, possible lawsuits and all associated. In conversation, it's often possible to dissuade less confident people from making the complaint, heading the whole thing off, before it starts.

---

298 https://en.wikipedia.org/wiki/Weapon_of_mass_destruction

The Algorithmic Anarchist   Hugh Barnard 24/10/21

Unconference[299]

In principle, this might be part of an entry on negotiation and discussion. To quote the Wikipedia entry 'An unconference is a participant-driven meeting. The term *unconference* has been applied, or self-applied, to a wide range of gatherings that try to avoid hierarchical aspects of a conventional conference.

These are participant driven conferences, in which most of the agenda and the organisation is done by the participants in the opening part of the conference. There are a variety of scopes and techniques.

For example, solving a particular problem or set of fairly well-defined problems in a specific area, health technology, for example. In this case there may be overlap with with coding and prototyping. Or broader, WSFII – World Summit on Free Information Infrastructures[300] in 2005 in Limehouse[301]. Actually the idea first appeared in political activism but has been used in open technology, a great deal.

Here's how a simple, usually one-day unconference works:
1. Participants arrive and create Post-It notes with their ideas
2. The notes are grouped into themes (as far as possible) on a wall
3. Everyone looks through the themes and sub themes, voting, if there's not enough time for everything.
4. The conference splits into tables or rooms for each theme, with someone reporting to the main conference towards the end of it.

---

299 https://en.wikipedia.org/wiki/Unconference
300 http://webarchive.okfn.org/okfn.org/201404/events/wsfii/
301 https://en.wikipedia.org/wiki/Limehouse

The Algorithmic Anarchist   Hugh Barnard 24/10/21

There are lots of variations on this and, probably, lots of scope for refinement. It is 'amusing' to note that the format is being recuperated and (badly) adapted by government organisations and hence by predatory suppliers of 'deliberative software', here's an example where, apparently UK civil servants went to Canada[302], to discuss, well who knows?

It's interesting to note that there's a fair amount of open source conference software but not a great deal done for unconferences, here's a list[303].

Lastly, Citizen's Assemblies[304] may have an unconference format and this may be healthier, if slightly more chaotic. Current 'official' experiments are a step in the right direction but tend to be tightly scoped to prevent wider discussions within. This is an area where I feel there are opportunities for a great deal of fruitful experiment, let a hundred flowers bloom[305].

---

302 https://www.oneteamgov.uk/global
303 http://olea.org/diario/2017/10/27/opensource-conference-management-software.html
304 https://en.wikipedia.org/wiki/Citizens%27_assembly
305 https://en.wikipedia.org/wiki/Hundred_Flowers_Campaign

The Algorithmic Anarchist	Hugh Barnard 24/10/21

Utopia

Actually that should probably be in the plural, Utopias, or maybe (if you're a modal person[306]) possible Utopias.

Marx wrote off the Utopians (one personal favourite is Fourier[307], who believed that the seas would be turned into lemonade) at the stage of the communist manifesto. Actually, Fourier may be partially correct, given steadily increasing carbon dioxide, the seas might change into fizzy water. Just add sugar, branding and advertising to make that a 'good' thing.

Marx didn't believe in raising living conditions for all, just for the proletariat. However, I believe that Utopias, even if unachievable, are a worthwhile thought experiment and tool for debate. They receive very little attention also in speculative literature because dramatically, they can be dull. Imagine a book with 'they lived happily ever after' on the very first page.

However, they answer the question 'If you had a clean slate and magical powers, what kind of world would you like to live in?' Secondly to recycle a cliché, the good is the enemy of the best, current governments and administrations usually concentrate on the 'least worst' or 'what we can get away with until we are out of office and become highly paid directors/consultants/speech-makers'.

---

306 https://plato.stanford.edu/entries/logic-modal/
307 https://en.wikipedia.org/wiki/Charles_Fourier

The Algorithmic Anarchist   Hugh Barnard 24/10/21

So, we need to sit, a few times a year thinking and discussing our own Utopias as a method to give direction to any smaller personal projects. For example, I grow fruit and vegetables because I believe 'freedom' is something to do with (and it's a complicated subject) not being beholden to large profit-oriented corporate systems. I do not mind being beholden and gifting to my neighbours, for example. Also, I buy very little or nothing using commercial credit from banks, if I haven't got the cash, I do without, most or all of it I don't 'need' anyway. So that's me, but others may have valid ideas that are 'not that'. The important thing is to have some argument and direction about the future, for both oneself and one's family.

Incidentally, I love Winstanley's slogan 'Glory Heere, Diggers All[308]'. Go him.

That's all folks, for this bit. Now read on.

---
308 https://mudcat.org/thread.cfm?threadid=120580,120580

The Algorithmic Anarchist   Hugh Barnard 24/10/21

Two Essays

Note: These essays were written in about 2010, when I lived on the Barleymow Estate in Limehouse.

Sense and Sensor Networks

Sorry, I tried to work that into something like Sense and Sensibilia, especially as I'm an Austin (but not Austen, I like Clueless though) fan. Next time, maybe, and all decent suggestions welcome at the usual address. I'll credit you too, though not in coin of the realm. This is a open workbook, as well as a rantbook, so you can contribute, if you like.

Introduction

There's been a lot of counter-intuitive but sensible talk about how cities are pretty good units of greenicity. I just made that up, but it describes what I'm after, in general. Cities are dense so that there's opportunities for efficient power generation with low transmission losses, short and optimised transport loops and small physical footprint living. We may not want to live in Japanese or Hong Kong sized boxes but if the 'outside' is a pleasant park, that could compensate. All this, actually supports fairly large populations, but probably doesn't feed them, a major outstanding problem.

The Algorithmic Anarchist   Hugh Barnard 24/10/21

The transport and travel loops provide an excuse to take an interest in graph theory, the travelling salesman problem and logistics, in general. Hurrah for Hamiltonians, they will help set us free! As usual, I don't intend to provide complete explanations of some of the technical stuff. You can do some work yourself and then claim credit for any ideas (you'll be anxious to do this, if you're a member of a conventional political party anyway) as your own. I don't 'want' them and I've probably got more, they're not scarce, just a quiet day and a scrap of paper will get you started. You may have to read a book or two and talk to a few people first though.

Back to the subject. Although cities are potentially 'good' units in this way, they are 'bad' units in many other ways. They generate sewage, airborne and water-borne pollution, poisoned top soil and concrete and tarmac crusts (due to the inner monologues of the status quo) at an alarming rate. They also generate noise pollution, low level crime, light pollution (linked to the fear of crime) and mental and physical illness. The mental and physical illness is the result of the other factors, though also somewhat self-inflicted. They are currently energy-hogs and heat sinks too.

A footnote, a lot of the actual waste is corporate, PCs powered up, lights left on, illuminated advertising and shop fronts. In spite of this, the government plays at (with the deep bad faith of the existential Sartreian sense) energy savings by nannying the citizen. The government can't turn on the corporates on behalf of the citizens (an act of good faith, probably) because they are part of the (in the situationist sense) show.

The Algorithmic Anarchist   Hugh Barnard 24/10/21

Sense and Measure

So the first thing to be done is to measure and show. By measure, I mean measure everything and I also mean 'overmeasure' (that is, not be satisfied with statistically significant samples, because they mask serendipity and extreme events) to do the job properly. Here are some of things that can be measured:

- airborne gas composition, especially the usual suspects
- airborne particulates
- sewage volumes and composition
- canal and river oxygenation and acidity
- aggregate energy usage (interesting since all supplies are in private hands)
- aggregate fossil fuel consumption

There's a lot of soft factors too, such as hospital admissions and low level crime. Traditionally these figures are worthless because they're massaged and used as political footballs. So perhaps we need vow-of-honesty measurement priests in charge of all this too. I'm sure that there's plenty missing and some things may turn out to be infeasible, this is an idea-in-progress. Although, I'm rabidly anti-neoclassical and don't like number fetishes (try silk, try leather there's a good situationist), there's some sense in making two or three fairly simple indexes out of these.

There's a large technology side-project here too. This needs within-reach evolution in sensing technology both in the breadth of what's being sensed, sensor features (all of them need to be networked) and price-point, since there are likely to be thousands of them. Some of this work is happening in universities, though, given the nauseating

The Algorithmic Anarchist   Hugh Barnard 24/10/21

connection imposed between learning and 'industry' by 'modern' politicians since Thatcher, a great deal of it will be closed by patents, NDAs and unproductive money maggots.

So, I'm assuming that a network of these sensors exists and the inputs can be aggregated, stored and displayed. The raw results, aggregates and trends should be free and available to everyone. This is open data in the style of the US Geographic Survey (but not, of course, our expensive paid-for-twice Ordinance Survey). This provides extra benefits in that enthusiasts will work with the data for free and perhaps discover useful correlations and trends. We didn't try crowd sourcing on green issues, a useful and exciting 'yet'.

We then have a picture of the vitals signs and trends for our city on a rolling, transparent and unmediated basis. How different this is from 'retail sales', 'consumer confidence' (how about citoyen ras-de-bol, look that up), 'GNP', 'unemployment figures' and other massaged stuff designed to frighten, manipulate and suck out our souls. No wonder that half our yoof spend the weekends getting hammered. We have a cyber-gaia snapshot.

Social Policy via Rewards

The next stage is to reward positive changes in the life-signs of the city by rewarding the inhabitants, Most of this is probably self-financing, since, for example, lower airborne pollution will result in lower hospital admissions and general levels of illness. Hey, people may be at work more and be more productive, the poor fools.

My emphasis in this, as in approaches to other problems in these essays is reward for merit, rather than punishment via taxation. This

The Algorithmic Anarchist   Hugh Barnard 24/10/21

is an idea borrowed from Professor Apichai and, in general, the Buddhist economists. If people do 'good' things, something should come back to them. The altruists and idealists will do things 'anyway' (the right reason) but the less-enlightened will do things for actual benefit. People see taxes as the 'cost of doing business' usually not as behaviour modifiers.

So, I would plan to issue social policy bonds, Ronnie Horesh's idea, for improvements to some of these indicators and indexes. Social policy bonds have a maturity value greater than issue, if the specific goal is fulfilled. Otherwise, for example, they would expire as worthless. Thus, the price will fall over their lifetime until, we hope, that people buy the specific issue and begin to solve the particular problem. It's important to avoid perverse effects, for example, it may be a little harsh to kill people that are littering, however much they really deserve it. We should be satisfied just with maiming them and tatooing 'ignorant littering oik' on their foreheads, if there was room.

It would be better if certain issues were exclusively community purchased (rather than by organisations or corporates) and therefore become a fields for action within a specific area or community. This is a detail though.

For example, quantities of kitchen waste can be removed at local level and turned into compost. There is already a reward to the council concerned for this, in the form of £40, and rising, per tonne of landfill tax that would not be payable. Thus, local composting can be self financing. However, councils love (other people's) money, so only rarely, and at election time, will they pass on such a saving. I'm currently doing some informal measuring work on my peelings to work out some figures for anaerobic composting for my estate. Currently Maidenhead and Versailles are offering some kind of reward based system. In Maidenhead, the rewards are consumer goods, how stupid!

If there's a bond for car journey levels, people can start to car share or use existing car share infrastructure. Some of them might even want to try walking or cycling too. The bonds have a specific objective not a specific method (bear in mind, perverse effects though).

Invent and Communicate

When approaching solutions, there'll be invention, trial and error, things that work well, things that people dislike and various combinations of all these elements. That's fun! It's exploration of the solution space or trying-things-out.

Since, we have the internet now, we can communicate some of these successes and failures to our cyber-neighbours who may be exploring solutions to the same kind of problems. They may have comments or improvements too. This is open knowledge in action, it doesn't require huge failed government projects or government intervention. Some of the approaches will fail but they will fail on a small scale leaving some good folk wisdom.

And That's It

That's all folks. We're nearly there with some of the initiatives but this is a more general approach. My intuition is that this is a good approach for small scale local initiatives because they are more sensitive to local conditions. I'm somewhat involved in the parish-council devolved democracy movement and this seems like a good approach at 'parish' (2K – 10K people, for example) level.

There's plenty wrong, for example, airborne pollution doesn't respect borough boundaries, though politicians would like to believe that.

The Algorithmic Anarchist   Hugh Barnard 24/10/21

A Green Micro-Economy

This is a second attempt at something I wrote about four years ago. According to a couple of non-expert views , the first one was interesting and also somewhat incomprehensible, so I'm taking a second run at it. It combines quite a few ideas in the other essays too, merit, recycling, complementary currencies and compost (like many people who were around in the 50s, I love compost more than anything, though not more than life itself, compost needs humans). So first, a few explanatory words and notes.

Introduction

First, a complementary currency is some kind of technology (paper notes, electronic exchange of numbers, large but very pretty stones with a hole in them) for storage and exchange of value. It is distinct from the national or regional (the euro, for example) currency, sometimes convertible but preferably not completely. By convertible, I'm talking about exchanging the complementary currency for a national or regional one. This is a complementary rather than alternative, the currency co-exists happily (we hope) with its larger (but more destructive) relation.

The currency, in this case, is a backed currency. A backed currency is exchangeable for some commodity or service. The simplest (and probably the most stupid but culturally very popular) are currencies that are backed by gold. There's not much you can do with gold, one can't eat it for example, you can make electronics and jewellery

The Algorithmic Anarchist   Hugh Barnard 24/10/21

from it. Gold is 'valuable' because a) it's scarce b) it's pretty, pretty thin reasons. In this economy, a commodity basket (a known mixture of useful stuff) is used to back the currency.

Second, merit. This is borrowed directly from the Buddhist idea of merit, particularly the 'sila' or virtue part. The virtue part covers 'good conduct' which I have westernised somewhat, and aimed outside the precepts. Also, merit can be transferred (I'm actually not too comfortable about this) in special circumstances. In the west, we have degenerate, deformed and monetised versions of this, in the form, for example of 'loyalty cards' or 'rewards'. It would be an amusing (that's not really the word I want, is it?) essay to see whether we have constructed a complete set-mapped degenerate and monetised version of some of the other concepts too.

I have reversed the usual western government procedure, that is, tax undesirable conduct in order to try and change it and (not coincidently) make a shed-load of money for the commissioning bureaucracy. Hurrah, the magic trough is always full! Also, as I've said elsewhere, these 'costs' are usually absorbed as the 'cost of doing business' or externalised (dumped by businesses onto individuals, mainly) whereas people are always happy with a 'bargain'. I'm thinking about positive feedback and virtuous circles rather than damping, for example. Finally, it's always worth turning anything on it's head, to provide extra insight. I'm not, of course, going to say that many politicians and bureaucrats should be stood on their heads and left there (the name of that rhetorical constructions is 'impatiens', for those that like that kind of thing).

The Economy Itself

Ok, I hope the more esoteric items are a little clearer, let's go to work. My complementary currency has three items backing it:

- some national currency, that comes from selling stuff created in the economy itself (endogenously, the big word)
- energy that's generated from biomass, CHP and photovoltaic
- compost that's produced from composting products

The currency serves about 320K people maximum, a big London borough

Let's start with the borough wide composting, which produces the following effects:

- provides free compost for the food growing within the circumference of the economy
- provides compost for sale, for national currency, outside the circumference
- reduce landfill and thus provides payback in reduced landfill tax
- reduce size, weight and frequency of garbage pickup, more credits

So, our happy subjects, who, by regaining some control over their lives, are starting to become citizens again, start to compost. Hey, I do this in my maisonette garden now, it's much, much smaller than a handkerchief.

The Algorithmic Anarchist   Hugh Barnard 24/10/21

You can either start to compost with communal compost heaps (which your council will hate) or anaerobic composters (which your council will love, capital expenditure, jobs for the lads, subcontracts, mmmmm!). However, you can compost quickly, higher volumes and greater range of stuff from large-scale anaerobic composters.

The solar cells, CHP and biomass (at the moment waste biomass from our horticultural 'contractor', good name, for a decent amount of money they kill and spray stuff, like their crime cousins) installations, provide a reasonable amount of electricity, generating credit values as the surplus goes back into the grid.

Finally, some community actions, such as delittering (meaning that the council is not paying expensive subcontractors and writing leaflets about it) are credited too.

Incidentally, as I've suggested in the s(n)ide remarks, unitary and borough councils are likely to hate this, it removes power, scarcity control (more power) and influence from the centre and moves it down a few notches. In fact, the correct within-the-system way to do this, may be via low-level parish, village or ward councils. These are possible now, even within the London boroughs.

Now, the commodity backing is being created, currency can be issued. Because national currency is only part of the backing, it isn't at the same value as (parity) with the national currency. This prevents, to some extent, value leaking from the currency catchment area. There's a certain amount of national currency 'pump priming', buying and installing solar cells and composters, for example. There's also, inevitably, some expense in national currency, maintenance, spare parts and specialized labour, for example.

The Algorithmic Anarchist   Hugh Barnard 24/10/21

The currency can now be issued in transparent and known quantities (unlike our current for-profit issued currencies, created at about 90% via bank debt). It's interesting to find a way to do this equitably, perhaps via equal (and by that I mean the same quantity) to every citizen in the currency boundary as (mutual or cooperative style) dividends. It's a nice piece of optimism to think that the rich would simply give away their dividend to someone else or to a local cause that uses the currency, perhaps they would. The currency then makes its way into the 'general' local economy, smaller shops and services, restoring some balance against the larger players. A small 'banking' and electronic transfer 'industry' springs up, if the currency is note/coin based.

Governance, issuance and withdrawal need some though. In general, there's temptation to fraud when the stakes are high and the risk/reward levels are looking good (complete convertibility and notes in large denominations, for example), a good reason for human-scale, perhaps the 250K population is too big? It might be useful, but limiting to restrict the whole currency to 'greening' transactions (seeds, tools, garden labour, saplings, compost and top soil, for example) and then widen its applicability to the 'general' local economy after a while. The limiting case of this is a token voucher or stamp which is only useful for one type of thing.

People can redeem certain quantities of currency for the national currency, but it won't be a good bargain, so they'll be encouraged to do things in the locality. It would be good to find a way to prevent supermarkets from accepting it too, perhaps via governance measures limiting redemption from certain types of organisation.

The Algorithmic Anarchist   Hugh Barnard 24/10/21

I'm not pretending that any of this is a precise schematic, there's a great deal to be blocked in, nice sacks for the compost, currency governance committee, green transport for moving stuff around, documentation and explanation, systems for currency transfer and auditing money supply against commodity levels, want/offer boards and volunteers at all levels. It's a thought adventure that needs to be brought to life.

I see some of this as being biomimetic (a word that's gradually becoming more popular, watch out) as mimicking some of the human body. We have systems that carry blood, lymph and nerve impulses, we don't have one, general nutrient, removal of interstitial fluid and signalling system all-mixed-up. This is a conceptual weakness of 'big' general purpose currency and a clue that smaller-scale specialised technologies -may- work better (unless you're a hypercapitalist who believes that everything from the classical economics was delivered on a stone tablet; well, a lot of it is certainly in indecipherable language). All of our economic systems and signals are mixed up (polluted or trafficked, some might say) in one unreasonable tangled large thingy used for everything from luxury cars (bad, mainly) to food (essential for human life) to seeds (good, in most cases).

We could, of course, make good decisions and account well for all this. This is one of the intuitions of 'carbon trading' and pollution trading (neither of which I believe in, they are mainly unenforceable, create privilege, greenwash and miss the point which is not to do it) for example, instruments and units of values can be specialised in a positive way.

We can broaden this out to a complete and distinct set of expressions for value linked, for example, to food, non-renewables,

The Algorithmic Anarchist   Hugh Barnard 24/10/21

renewables, energy and things-that-we-don't-really-want. This is great but there's always the problem of convertibility and leakages, food stamps to cigarettes, already tends to happen, for example. I'm hoping that the transition towns in the UK will take some of this approach when they think about local money rather than going for parity and convertibility with the national currency, running to stand still, really.

Cover It All With Green

When I'm in Bangkok, arguably more problematic in governance and transparency than Tower Hamlets, I spend some of my time taking pictures of street vegetation. Same thing in Singapore, I'm a carbon criminal, but I get around.

One day, I will show some of these pictures to someone in the council, if I can find someone actually working for the good of the borough. In fact, there are plenty, but they're never very senior, never will be, can't stop the top floor gravy train can we?

These pictures are of planters, lane dividers on the edges of pavements and pretty much everywhere. Singapore also has flowers hanging or on shelves on the pedestrian bridges and Bangkok is beginning to follow suit (the mayor of Bangkok went to Singapore to take a look, a fine example of being able to learn, must be something missing in the water here). Lastly, on the Sky Train support pillars there are cheap lightweight trellises with climbing plants, so the climbers cover the pillars without eroding them.

The Algorithmic Anarchist　　　Hugh Barnard 24/10/21

So, this is a complete vertical and horizontal program that could be pushed much further for very little cash, trellis work everywhere, vegetation and micro-agriculture on roofs, concrete pillars and (ugly) walls, hiding them from view and making them inaccessible to graffiti. The school of management in Singapore has vegetation overflowing from its balconies too, looking out from Sukhumvit 8 over (affluent) Bangkok, this is beginning to happen there as well.

It's fairly low cost too, trellis from recycled plastic (though watch out for UV damage if uncovered), water from rainfall (though our 'gubbiment' prefers us to pay their mates for it) and some low-value (in a 'market' environment, shame it's more noble than banking, for example) labour.

I've called the food part, the CIA, the Campaign for Interstitial Agriculture. It's an idea, a meme but, starting with Cuba, there are great sprouts of it everywhere, gardenshare, fruit up front etc.

I live near an ugly, busy, urban, old fashioned four lane highway which would benefit from this approach. The cost is probably in the region of tens of thousand too, but, instead we 'choose' (well Coe-baby, a load of property developers and some gassy idea-free politicians choose for us) to waste about £20bn on the 'Olympics'. Yes, I know it's £10bn (up from £2bn) but it'll come out to about £20bn, you'll see, especially when we start importing US security 'consultants' to keep us 'safe'.

The Algorithmic Anarchist   Hugh Barnard 24/10/21

Now, the next thing is more radical. We need to remove the vast swathes of tarmac, concrete and paving and replace them with wildflower drifts, lawn and smallish sheep tracks (for wet days). There are huge pieces near me (in a park and around the Limehouse basin) not justified by any significant traffic. Of course, now they are there, they are used for 'parking' and riding bicycles too fast. Walking and cycling needs to capture a reversal of the Good Roads Movement (which started with bicycles anyway).

Tarmac is a heat sink, an eyesore, an incitement to speed (in the future we won't need clocks, recycle a couple now, as a gesture), doesn't absorb $C0_2$ or compost, unpleasant to the eye and prevents natural run-off. What good is it, everywhere? Same remark for paving stones, although these, at least have a bit of built-in run-off. We need some tarmac but a great deal less. I'm fine with some road transport, but we need to reduce the addiction and be more logistics-minded as a pervasive policy, to the devil with gassy ($C0_2$ being the gas) special interest groups like the RAC foundation.

As the title says, cover it with green, you have nothing to lose but your tarmac and concrete surfaces. We can measure the success or failure of this policy too, since it's got a a surface area. Hey, we're almost back to the days of window tax! Except that this is better done with some kind of local incentive such as social policy bonds or local credits of some kind.

Of course, our council tends to move in the other direction, more and more tarmac. There is a simple reason for this, the horticulture is subcontracted, so the less that has to be done (mowed, trimmed, planted or weeded), the greater the profit for the subcontractor. Did I mention that most of the subcontracts are 'partership agreement' subcontracts, murky things that deliver unquantified benefits for the

The Algorithmic Anarchist   Hugh Barnard 24/10/21

council and very little for the tax or service charges payer? Thus, there's pockets to be filled and money to be made from tarmac, before, during and after.

We had a small area on Pennyfields (E14) that was fine for football, using, as a friend said, sweaters and tops for goalposts. That has been turned, at a cost of about £100K into a tarmac floored cage, which is now useful for 'sport'. Another example of grant-fueled uselessness. Actually I've just seen another in the east of the borough too, and, we have the same thing on our estate.

It represents about four unthinking steps in the wrong direction. First, there's nothing wrong with sport on grass, that's where it usually takes place. Second, these things do no need to be fenced in completely. Third, they do not need fixed goal posts (or even basketball goals, they can go up and come down), as my friend said, sweaters and tops will be enough. Fourth, after these three steps, high fencing will not be necessary, because there'll be nothing fixed to climb into.

There's a situationist thread that connects with this, the idea of psychogeography. Some of the reasoning that led to the pedestrianisation of Les Halles (the old fruit and vegetable wholesale market in the centre of Paris, now moved to the suburbs so that more petrol can be used, a triumph for the idea of 'real estate' and 'shopping malls') were based on this. Meanwhile, the greener the city looks, the greener it gets, barring Potemkin villages covered with institutional green paint.

The Algorithmic Anarchist   Hugh Barnard 24/10/21

Library 451[309]:

Fit the First[310]: Looking for 'books'

This saga started quite innocently and very uncontroversially. I wanted to donate some expensive, slightly out-of-date technical books to Newham library. This, on the basis of new skills and hobbies in a borough that always needs them. All donations were refused.

I was told that the selection of books and management of them was via a third party and that I couldn't donate. I thought that's 'interesting' and left the whole subject for a while, concentrating on other things. Also, I'd scoured (on the basis of several years earlier, in Tower Hamlets) the shelves for IT books of 'substance' Code Complete[311], Applied Crytography[312], and Software Engineering[313], say. Or something on Linux, open source tools and other (my phrase, pace Illich[314]) 'technologies of liberation'. After all, in principle, Newham is a Labour borough and 'therefore' a socialist borough. What I actually found on the shelves was Mac for Dummies, Excel for Dummies etc. etc. nothing challenging or educative. I'm not against these particular books but not as a exclusive diet.

---
309 I can't find *this*, either, another reason for title.
310 I can't find *this*, either.
311 https://en.wikipedia.org/wiki/Code_Complete
312 https://en.wikipedia.org/wiki/Bruce_Schneier#Publications
313 https://en.wikipedia.org/wiki/Ian_Sommerville_(software_engineer)
314 https://en.wikipedia.org/wiki/Ivan_Illich

Next, I broadened my investigation to fiction and other categories. I couldn't find any Dostoevsky, Faulkner, Hesse or Kafka for example, searching through fiction alphabetically as a sad person might do. Incidentally, I'm not a reading snob and read an enormous quantity of detective fiction especially during the winter months. In politics, I could find only a few books and some mis-shelved, since this is a 'socialist' borough, I'd expect In Place of Fear[315], for example and, at least some kind of Marx introductory reader, Marx for Beginners (Rius, this is pretty good, actually), even.

What I did find here was best sellers (AKA high-promoted by publishers), (YA) young adult, and chick lit. All of these on the 'promotional' new books tables. I have nothing against any of these but they are not a complete diet. Broccoli as well as chocolate biscuits.

Some Twitter exchanges followed, patronising on their side, that they were happy for members of the public to make 'suggestions' (that presumably they would studiously ignore, I didn't try, see Fit the Second).

---

315 https://en.wikipedia.org/wiki/Aneurin_Bevan

Fit the Second: Interrogating the 'library'

Now it was time to a) get an overview of the complete Newham stock and b) find out about the third party. With regard to stock, I'm maintaining a distinction between a) stock in the murky multi-borough system b) shelved permanently in Newham c) promoted on tables etc.

In (fairly) good faith, I thought about the idea of 'suggestions', however, before making any I wanted an overview of the catalogue and what's already regularly available in the borough, so that I was not duplicating existing stock. Some curiosity, as well, that thing about the cat is *fake news*.

So here's the FOI request[316] for the catalogue. Here are some extracts from the reply. I've amended the status to refused, since effectively they're doing that by prevaricating:

It is not possible to recover a CSV file of the complete book catalogue from our library management system. In an attempt to comply with your request, contact has been made with the suppliers of this system to enquire as to whether conversion to a CSV file may be possible. As you noted in your request, the numbers of entries run into the hundreds of thousands, to be extracted from the full multi-borough catalogue of eight million titles across London.

---

316 https://www.whatdotheyknow.com/request/request_for_library_catalogue#incoming-1672858

The Algorithmic Anarchist			Hugh Barnard 24/10/21

Incidentally, I've redone my calculation for 8 million records this is about 500Mb for the extract. It'll fit on a small USB stick. And then:

```
Despite a number of attempts, the suppliers have
confirmed it is not possible to complete this
exercise without further extensive work on the
conversion of the data, to include each of the
four headings of information per title entry
requested, to a server and then compilation of
multiple reports
```

I actually have some sympathy with this, it's probably a problem created by Marc[317], an ancient standard, developed in the USA. TL:DR

```
The future of the MARC formats is a matter of some
debate among libraries. On the one hand, the storage
formats are quite complex and are based on outdated
technology. On the other, there is no alternative
bibliographic format with an equivalent degree of
granularity. The billions of MARC records in tens of
thousands of individual libraries (including over
50,000,000 records belonging to the OCLC consortium
alone) create inertia.
```

However, my sympathy is limited by this[318], for example. There are almost certainly other programming libraries too. They probably didn't try *very hard*, after all, I am just a *member of the public* and a *resident*. I didn't send this to the Information Commissioner *yet*.

---

317 https://en.wikipedia.org/wiki/MARC_standards
318 https://metacpan.org/pod/MARC::Record

The Algorithmic Anarchist   Hugh Barnard 24/10/21

But the upshot is, apparently, according to Newham Libraries, no-one has a decent overview of the complete catalogue. Probably, I didn't try this, no-one has an overview of section, politics or philosophy, let's say?

Next, the inaccessible catalogue is being managed (and run?) for multiple boroughs using (in my opinion) clunky, closed source American software[319]. Incidentally, SirsiDynix is now owned by ICV Partners, an American private equity company, so I doubt there will be much innovation, since private equity is usually and essentially extractive.

SirsiDynix, apparently, isn't a big open source fan either:

```
On October 29, 2009, the WikiLeaks Project obtained a
document from SirsiDynix taking a negative view of
open source projects as compared to proprietary
products, including risks of instability and
insecurity.
```

Why would they, private equity doesn't have a notion of public good, does it? Can't make high returns from it either.

Next, since the shelved, promoted and 'visible' part of the library is full of unchallenging *mush* (I'm exaggerating slightly), who or what is choosing these books?

---
319 https://en.wikipedia.org/wiki/SirsiDynix

The Algorithmic Anarchist   Hugh Barnard 24/10/21

The answer is, drum roll, Collection HQ[320][321], *the world's leading collection performance improvement solution.* They use Evidence Based Stock Management[322], in a (several) words, *never mind the quality, feel the width.* This is essentially, I believe, algorithmic, based on checkouts, sales popularity and other indicators. However, since the algorithm(s?) are hidden in proprietary closed source software, this is informed speculation on the matter.

This is the Newham FOI[323] on the actually selection procedure, which doesn't reveal very much, except a great many meetings. It is also (apparently) is mainly concentrated on new publications, rather than the ambition to have a well balanced catalogue with shelved books from a selection of non-YA, non-chicklit, non-Dummies. This list[324], for example, might be a 'start', lots more work to do here though.

I've also made a distinction between 'held', 'shelved' (but where?) and 'promoted', since the library has used a certain amount of sophistry around 'held' (somewhere in the system in some participating borough, not good enough). Most of what is promoted is, in fact, *mush.*

---

320 https://www.collectionhq.com/
321 On April 18, 2016 Follett Corporation announced their acquisition of Baker & Taylor (owners of CollectionHQ). Follett is a top provider of technology, services and print and digital content to PreK-12 libraries, schools and higher education institutions.
322 The methodology comprises of a framework that guides practitioners through a phased journey towards *collection performance excellence. What does that even mean?*
323 https://www.whatdotheyknow.com/request/673683/response/1617707/attach/html/4/817230%20FOI%20RESPONSE.pdf.pdf.html
324 https://markmanson.net/best-books/nonfiction

The Algorithmic Anarchist   Hugh Barnard 24/10/21

Fit the Third: Where We Are Now

Meanwhile, in summary:

- We have a closed source, US based and private equity owned library management system that apparently we are locked in to.

- We are unable to take an overview of the whole catalogue, somewhat essential for making balanced decisions and adding and completing the stock

- To some extent, at least, new additions are suggested by a closed algorithmic process owned by a US based digital company with its focus mainly based in the USA

The result is abysmal for broad culture but especially civics and political theory in the borough. We already have high apathy and abstention, we're clearly working on abolishing reasoned choice too. That's apart from the hole where good literature might be, partially controlled and burnt by America's Library 451[325].

---

325 Fahrenheit 451. You guessed it though, didn't you? In later years, he described the book as a commentary on how mass media reduces interest in reading literature.[7]

The Municipal Green Opportunity

Note:This was first presented as a final year essay for my philosophy BA finished in 2019.

Analytic philosopher: let's simplify this to the point it has no relation to the problem. Continental philosopher: let's complicate this to the point no one understands it. - Existential Comics

Undoing and replacing the national neo-liberal climate narrative, both project and philosophy at municipal level.

Introduction

This essay argues that current national, top-down technocratic policies guided partially by the economics of the 'market' will fail (partially or disastrously) to mitigate or build resilience toward a rapidly changing climate. It proposes and argues, in its stead, for local initiatives and solutions framed by a green holistic narrative.

Conventional analytic philosophy posits the primacy of ideal model ethical and thence political theories upon which to base policy and the conduct of government. In this essay, I follow Geuss[i] who, in my opinion, makes a sharp and successful regress attack on a number of systems of ideal theory based ethics.

The Algorithmic Anarchist   Hugh Barnard 24/10/21

Following Geuss, I emphasise the contextual and the contingent, thus finding myself adrift from the purely analytic and steering, in my post-Neurathian boat (ship's master Captain Quine), towards the sociology of imaginaries[326] and of Utopia as method[ii]. I conclude with a partial sketch of a resilient municipality, somewhat following (later ideas of) Bookchin[iii] a model that, I believe, can be achieved at municipal level rather than from central government as in the two competing and (as I argue, failing) cases that I have called Standard Technocratic and Reactive.

There is a very extensive bibliography since I hope that this essay will be a stimulus to further and deeper reading and (perhaps) action by some of my local political actors.

Scope of the Discussion

This essay took as a starting point, my borough in London, that is therefore, paradoxically, given the above, also somewhat an *ideal* model, since it only deals with part of one city. One can immediately argue that this is imperfect since interactions at the boundaries, for example violent incursion, unhappily there is no valid response here, without writing a book instead of an essay.

---

326 The imaginary (or social imaginary) is the set of values, institutions, laws, and symbols common to a particular social group and the corresponding society through which people imagine their social whole.

The Algorithmic Anarchist   Hugh Barnard 24/10/21

Three Failures and Three Approaches

I focus on, *water and food supply* and *public health*. For example, there will certainly be flooding at the lower levels and near waterways, but these problems are localised and bounded. In contrast, food supply and public health concern all ages, genders, and circumstances, though the poor, young, old and voiceless will, intuitively, have the worst of it.

For each, I discuss three political settings[327][iv], the the Standard Technocratic, the Reactive and the Green Libertarian Municipal (abbreviated GLM), with an emphasis on the latter. I de-emphasise the Reactive, for reasons that become clearer later. For GLM, which I favour, I argue from, the probable partial failure of central government technocratic resilience and mitigation[v]. In the first two, I have assumed that the municipal follows the national setting very closely, they are therefore top-down models, and in GLM that there are some elements of 'divorce' and active subsidiarity.

The technocratic setting is any centrist government from the late 20th and early 21st centuries. It implies a framework of neo-classical economics, using opportunity cost, equilibrium equations, intensive (and successful) lobbying by vested interests, identifying and satisfying 'consumers' and the other steps that we take when we try (not) to solve societal problems. I argue that this approach can tend to morph (or degenerate, to use more partisan language) into the Reactive.

---

327 I have called these *settings* because municipality sits within a broader political and societal landscape (unless we revert to autonomous city states and principalities). I have resisted *scenario,* pace Herman Kahn (see endnote d).

The Reactive is minimally and reactively interventionist, laissez-faire and could be described (or criticised) as right libertarian, minimal state. There would be (both metaphorically and literally) some fire fighting, but response only to serious threat or disorder only, no notions of of resilience or mitigation, remedy or distributive justice, for example. Response to threat, may, for example, consist of threat to the food or water supply of *current authority* or refusal to *tithe* or *be taxed*. Elements of this may be present, even in the absence of any recognisable contemporary institutions, for example, Somalia under the tribes and warlords.

Finally, GLM treats all policy strands as part of an ecologically sensitive framework and project, thus subsuming the two chosen problems (and the rest, but that is a longer text) into a greater whole. I assume, also, that some of the current institutions still exist, something that is, by no means, certain. However, the societal part of the GLM approach is based on building, rebuilding or strengthening low level institutions, such as citizen's assemblies, spaces for activity and reflection, and local co-operatives and non-profits, these are detached from the national political and economic setting but connected amongst themselves via well-defined systems of federation.

There are (at least!) two overarching questions for this approach. First are the chosen problems connected? For example, expensive and scarce food will clearly have an impact on public health. Following this line, if many of these problems are connected, does this favour GLM style approaches, since the proposed solutions are more integrated? I hope to be able to argue and answer in the affirmative, but so does technocratic government, in principle[328].

---

328 The net-zero challenge must be embedded and integrated across all

The second is about the relationship between the models. First, I am aware, that (pace David Lewis[vi]) there are many models that I have *not* treated. I have chosen three as being as what Lewis would style 'near' (near our current experience, laws of physics apply, all men are mortal), rather than *unicorn and chocolate fountain* worlds or, more traditionally The Land of Cockaigne[329]. I assume, that bits of the future are embedded in the present and the near future is 'recognisable', to quote William Gibson 'the future is here already, it is just unevenly distributed'. Without disappearing down a giant rabbit hole of symbolic and formal modality, these three models are considered to be related as in this quote[vii]:

> Another interpretation of the 'accessibility relation' with a physical meaning, the claim "is possible in the world is interpreted as "it is possible to transform into a world in which is true"

Adding, with a minimal (but unspecified) number of transformations. So, I believe that the three models are 'near', that they will transform, in some cases from one to another. However, in my view there are asymmetries, in that the Standard Technocratic model *can* transform into the Reactive (easily) or GLM (more difficult), but I do not believe that the Reactive model transforms easily, into either of the other two.

---

departments, at all levels of Government and in all major decisions that impact on emissions. **It must also be integrated with businesses and society at large.** *Since many of the solutions cut across systems, fully integrated policy, regulatory design and implementation is crucial* from: Various. (2019). Net Zero – The UK's contribution to stopping global warming.

329 A land of plenty in medieval myth, where physical comforts and pleasures are always immediately at hand and the harshness of medieval peasant life does not exist.

The GLM model *can* convert back into the Standard Technocratic but part of its 'design' (hopefully) makes it more unlikely to convert into the Reactive. I discuss some of the detailed changes that may effect transformation, when I discuss the models.

Argument

In our lives, we 'prepare', we get educated, save money and repair our homes. In all of these, we are making implicit, inductive assumptions about a somewhat unknowable future. We expect the same from our elected and paid officials, that there will be a national health service and a pension, if we fulfil certain conditions. All these assumptions are predicated on a central assumption *and hope* of a smooth and continuous path into the future.

However, let us suppose that we predict and prepare for significant discontinuities. There *will* be a sea battle tomorrow[viii] and it will decide whether our town is destroyed and we are sold into slavery, or not. This asymmetry is present in preparation for climate change too, the worst may not happen, in which case will our preparation be 'wasted'? I will argue that this is not so, as the joke[330] goes, we will not have constructed a much better world for 'nothing'. Climate change and its remedies are not like the sea battle either, there may be partial effects, partial change, a much more varied set of future scenarios.

---

330 James Governor. (2010). What If We Create a Better World For Nothing?.Available: http://greenmonk.net/2010/01/07/what-if-we-create-a-better-world-for-nothing/. Last accessed 29th October 2018.

The Algorithmic Anarchist   Hugh Barnard 24/10/21

In pure analytic philosophy, climate change might require, for example, a 'duty to prepare' as a collective responsibility, difficult in practice and full of hidden controversy[ix]. My alternative to an ideal theory of ethics is to be more modest and start from the two tiers at the bottom of Maslow's Hierarchy[331] (physiological and safety, see the footnote for a short explanation) on the basis that if we do not survive, there is, in fact, no discussion to be had.

Survival *transcends*, if we happen to believe that the human race is not a bad thing, another essay in itself. I believe this to be more in line with Raymond Geuss' criticism of the conduct of policy[x] having no direct relation to abstract ethical and political theories that take centre stage in analytic philosophy. Part of my approach here therefore is a contextual, *it's a mess but we'll do our best.*

What will Happen?

To anchor the rest, we need to understand what will happen to water and food supplies and public health in a time of changing climate. Already, this is a future contingent, it has the status of a partially evidenced, inductive thought experiment. Within there are two aspects of note, *conventional uncertainty* and *chaotic effects*. I only argue within 2-3°C changes, supported, for example by current IPCC studies and arguments.

---

331 Wikipedia contributors. (N.D.). Maslow's hierarchy of needs. Available: https://en.wikipedia.org/wiki/Maslow%27s_hierarchy_of_needs. Last accessed 29th October 2017. Maslow's hierarchy of needs is used to study how humans intrinsically partake in behavioural motivation. Maslow used the terms "physiological," "safety," "belonging and love," or "social needs" "esteem," and "self-actualization" to describe the pattern through which human motivations move.

Chaotic effects are, for example, unexpected increase in greenhouse gases (for example, unexpected release of buried methane hydrate[xi]) or non-linear increase in warming from substantial ice melts and consequent loss of reflective surface (albedo effects). It is not clear what will happen to weather patterns here, but the results are unlikely to be *good*, for humans, anyway. Chaotic effects are usually towards the *worse* rather than the *better* in this case, with the possible exception of persistent volcanic eruption leading to a volcanic winter, see [xii] [332]. But, even here, areas affected are unpredictable, crop loss is predicted, and increased ocean acidification is a side effect.

Finally, at 6°C[xiii], we're doomed anyway, so logically, this is not worth discussing, since the problem has *solved* itself, in a traditional way via a mass extinction.

Food Supply

I have used government statistics here[xiv] and here[xv], to provide the facts and arguments in this section. First, over 50% of UK food is imported, therefore we can potentially add (internal and external) political and logistical effects to climate effects. Second, we may also want to make more fine-grained arguments about dietary mix in the course of arguing about food.

---

[332] A volcanic winter is a reduction in global temperatures caused by volcanic ash and droplets of sulfuric acid and water obscuring the Sun and increasing reflection of solar radiation after a large, volcanic eruption.

The Algorithmic Anarchist — Hugh Barnard 24/10/21

The UK is not nearly self-sufficient as regards food, this article[xvi] discusses food security and Brexit, a good proxy for climate change stress and disruption. Food supply and diet are intimately linked to public health, in a number of ways, food shortages, calorific under nutrition, dietary deficiencies being the most obvious. Water, of course, sustains food production and we die quickly without it.

I therefore assume that we lose most of our imports, since our neighbours and suppliers will have the same scarcity and harvest problems and, logically and politically favour their local populations. If they do not and there is still some semblance of democracy, the population will be tempted to elect a government that does so. If there's no or little democracy (see the Reactive thread) the food will be hijacked (see Somalia) or traded away via corruption, so it will not arrive, either way.

Which native crops are most susceptible to climate change, since this is the second major factor in the 'reduced food mix'? Here are two sources[xvii][xviii] from the UK government and civil service. Maize and wheat, therefore bread and common types of meat (maize is used for cattle feed) will probably spike. We lose vegetables too, and putting water stress back into the equation, we see that the fruit and vegetable localism advocated later in the GLM approach makes sense in both contexts[xix] (loss of imports and climate based water stress). We will certainly eat less meat, whether we wish to or not.

The Algorithmic Anarchist   Hugh Barnard 24/10/21

Public Health

I have chosen to concentrate on physical health, although it is clear that there are consequences for mental health also. It is, however, much harder to speculate about mental health, except for a blanket, forward view that it may be generally 'worse', the evidence from the second world war, seems to suggest this[xx]. So, there are groups of problems, that are connected in many cases:

- Dietary problems from sub-optimal food supply
- Direct effects of heat, exhaustion, especially very young and very old
- Expensive drinking water
- Novel diseases and dangers enabled by a changing climate
- Unquantifiable mental stresses associated with the above factors

This leads to problems of access given (currently, as of 2018) already overburdened health resources. We have seen this already, excess death figures in France for recent summers[xxi], however there is some controversy about cause.

Solutions

I discuss the approaches here, in the order of Standard Technocratic coupled with Reactive and then move to GLM. I attempt to show, that Reactive and the Standard Technocratic solutions are likely to fail, since climate change is both a persistent and wicked[xxii] problem rather than a set of separate, separately solvable, orthogonal problems that would yield to organisations and narratives that are structured in governmental or organisational silos.

Also, intuitively, if any of the separate problems (or a subset) produces a sufficient level of societal dissatisfaction, then, a flashpoint may make the Standard Technocratic spiral down towards a Reactive, where any policy or preparation is abandoned for reaction and coercion. This is why I couple these two approaches, without any delight, if I were to be right.

Standard Technocratic

We can describe this as *business as usual*, many stable European countries look rather like this. Calculations are made using the formulae of neo-classical economics, the 'future' is discounted as a single number and food and healthcare are rationed using complex forms and esoteric calculations. There may be preparatory elements (Net Zero[xxiii], currently), but since they are compared to business as usual using opportunity cost, they are likely to be minimal. John Broome has provided a great deal of work[xxiv], taking this approach. It is noteworthy and alarming, for example, that any levels of preparation and mitigation depend on the discount rate chosen, usually framed in purely monetary terms[333].

---

333 Present value, also called "discounted value," is the current worth of a future sum of money or stream of cash flow given a specified rate of return. Future cash flows are discounted at the discount rate; the higher the discount rate, the lower the present value of the future cash flows.

The Algorithmic Anarchist   Hugh Barnard 24/10/21

The exercise is top down and full of esoteric terms and copious footnotes. For example, this paper on Ecosystem Based Adaptation[xxv] (EBA). Even at the lower level of a single country, Germany, the focus and level of concrete thinking improves somewhat[xxvi], but we are still in a technocratic quagmire[xxvii]. It is notable here that, looking at Figure 6 in reference 19, there has been no thought about mitigation for uncertain food supply. Technocratic society, our current model has a predominantly market narrative, therefore we can expect price spikes and volatility, in the absence of real scarcity (the sums *really* do not add up, we *actually* cannot feed everyone, as opposed to *some people do not have money*).

At the time of writing, there is a UK price spike for some medicines, one can expect some of the WHO essentials[xxviii] to spike too. This suggests a descent into the Reactive, one common cause of rioting is scarce or expensive food, especially in conditions of visible inequality[xxix]. Fuel prices are also a common cause of civil disturbance, UK fuel blockades[xxx] and from 2018 onwards, the French Gilets Jaunes. In 2017 in the UK, there were *telephone calls to the police* about a shortage of fried chicken, no words.

Worse, I agree with John O'Neill here[xxxi], we have a view partially framed by Ecosystem Services, in my view a mistaken and arrogant view of our planet, it uses a one dimension and monetary values for items which are a) incommensurable, no two trees are alike b) a tree has a complete micro-ecosystem with it and a relationship with other organisms, including nearby trees[xxxii] c) If science is even partially correct, this is Russian roulette, removing the 'last tree'[334] tips us from climate change into runaway climate tragedy.

---

334 When the last tree is cut, the last fish is caught, and the last river is polluted; when to breathe the air is sickening, you will realize, too late, that wealth is not in bank accounts and that you can't eat money - Alanis Obomsawin

The Algorithmic Anarchist   Hugh Barnard 24/10/21

In my view, to be broader and more philosophical, this kind of thinking is one of the larger negative intellectual externalities of the Enlightenment. Actually Marlowe warned us about this, well before the Enlightenment, making his Dr Faustus say *'Sweet Analytics 'tis thou has ravished me'*. Neitzsche, though ranting somewhat[335], saw this as a clear and present danger. Or, from the right, Edmund Burke[xxxiii]: *"The lines of morality are not like ideal lines of mathematics. They admit of exceptions; they demand modifications. These exceptions and modifications are not made by the process of logic, but by the rules of prudence."*

This approach leaves us with no clear, GLM or coherent governmental narrative, just a jumble of 'funding pots' and 'initiatives'. There are elements of Thatcherism's kitchen economics, *making numbers balance* as a philosophical good, numbers, outputs, and outcomes[336]. From bitter experience, outputs and outcomes are open to persistent fraud, anyway, remember the Russian (in the time of Союз Советских Социалистических Республик) joke, *'So long as the bosses pretend to pay us, we will pretend to work'*. A critic may (rightly) complain at this point that the Third Reich narrative was clear and, apparently, attractive. I try to partially answer this in the GLM section.

---

335 So far there has been no philosopher in whose hands philosophy has not grown into an apology for knowledge; on this point, at least, every one is an optimist, that the greatest usefulness must be ascribed to knowledge. They are all tyrannized over by logic, and this is optimism in its essence.

336 Outputs are the story of what you produced or activities. Output measures do not address the value or impact of your services. An outcome is the level of performance or achievement that occurred because of these activity or services.

The Algorithmic Anarchist   Hugh Barnard 24/10/21

That narrative void is supplied by Debord's Spectacle[xxxiv], a world saturated with artificial desires and life lived via proxies, especially via the narrative of competition (Bake Off, Strictly Come Dancing and assorted billionaires), happiness advertised as consumption and therefore debt.

Also something that I choose to call 'transactionalism'[337], reification's evil cousin, as I write this someone is making a business out of hugging people[xxxv]. Both the competition and the increasing orientation towards transaction, prepare and prefigure something more divisive and dystopian too.

Both radical left wing accelerationists[338] and Neitzsche actually support this tendency, in the hope that the system will finally fly apart, leaving room for the 'new'. However, things that fly apart usually leave wreckage, rather than shiny new things.

But, a critic may exclaim, the complex rules and regulations in (say) Universal Credit and Housing Benefit promote distributive 'fairness' and are therefore an ethical good, pace Rawls. Well, no, complexity is exclusionary, since those most in need are the least able to navigate the thicket of rules towards their legitimate benefits.

---

337 This is a much smaller-grained concept than financialisation. It is nearer Lefebvre's concept of 'colonisation', the permanent intrusion of profit-motivated consumption into the *minutiae* of 'everyday life'.
338 In political and social theory, accelerationism is the idea that the prevailing system of capitalism should be expanded fast in order to generate radical social change.

Last, although within this approach there is some space for mitigation, as we see from the cited EBA papers, the majority of initiatives are from the top downwards. Thus, they are often attenuated to the point of ineffectiveness by a version of the Cantillon Effect[339], roughly money injected into an economy will a) spread unevenly b) be of maximum benefit at the point of injection, in this case project 'management' rather than any useful part of the project. Mitigation itself is mitigated to the point of ineffectiveness.

Finally, we also note in the UK papers a need for *cross cutting* approaches, a tacit meta-admission that the technocratic silos cannot capture and mitigate this kind of pervasive and (pace Kuhn) paradigm altering problem.

Reactive Intervention

We can summarise this approach by exclaiming 'shoot all the (food) rioters!'. There are no substantial attempts at mitigation, rather any crisis is allowed to resolve itself, except when the current set of *haves* (who may rotate, see below) are threatened. The shooting above and other incidents of violence, racketeering and intimidation occur as part of the process, in the worst case, as a permanent societal feature.

---

339 The Cantillon Effect refers to the change in relative prices resulting from a change in money supply. The change in relative prices occurs because the change in money supply has a specific injection point and therefore a specific flow path through the economy. The first recipient is in the convenient position of being able to spend extra dollars *before* prices have increased.

The Algorithmic Anarchist   Hugh Barnard 24/10/21

There is an existing contemporary narrative accompanying this approach pushed by right libertarian, (often) Christian fundamentalist lobbyists (they often self-style as think tanks[xxxvi]), roughly, the best state is the most minimal state, the rich are rich because they are virtuous, the poor are feckless or morally defective and deep inequality is, in fact and paradoxically, equitable, some ghosts of Nozick's well-paid baseball player, repudiated here[xxxvii].

Also, since they are financed in part by fossil fuel interests, climate change is not happening. Worse, following Naomi Klein's concept of 'disaster capitalism'[xxxviii], there is a significant group who hope to profit from this disorder and oppose any form of mitigation. The collapse of the Soviet Union also made this type of opportunism surface, so it can be argued that this is a 'narrative of greed' rather than stemming from any particular political ideology.

There are some elements of this in current UK policy, for example, massive reduction of police and hospital spending, because, or as pretext, *the books must balance* (except for banks, however, who receive ample quantitative *easing*, to ease their pain, the magic money tree money whose delicious fruits are served often but only at the right tables), leading to a dysfunctional version of a Nozick style minimal state, to quote:

At one end of the spectrum are outlaw agencies or rogue individuals who either aim to perform actions that cross boundaries or pose substantial risks of crossing boundaries through their recklessness or negligence. The actions of such agencies or individuals may simply be suppressed to protect the rights that they threaten.

The Algorithmic Anarchist   Hugh Barnard 24/10/21

Under the stressors of popular food shortages (bread, for example, via cereal shortages), expensive fuel, water, and price spikes, broken public services, a discontented, and unequal population, it is reasonable to expect outlaw agencies and rogue individuals to appear and fill the gap left by legitimate (somewhat legitimate, there are no binary measures, pace Professor Wolff[xxxix]) agencies and individuals. Indeed, ordinal legitimacy may pass to ad-hoc groups, a form of institutional renewal, this is partly the basis of pre-emptive strengthening for local social bonds, argued later in the GLM section. But better via considered preparation and mitigation, than via chaos. This is an inductive but plausible conclusion, looking at black markets during UK wartime, especially World War II, recently Somalia or Venezuela burdened by US sanctions.

A pessimistic view grants a clear path from business as usual, given enough stress to a Reactive State and thence to failed (Somalia, DRC). For example, scarcity of necessities, price spikes and volatility, inequality, perceived injustice, perceived political illegitimacy and environmental stress.

We can add draconian laws, manipulation of media and civil authority excesses. It is a sinister truth that this path is continuous[xl], not discrete, there are no definitive distinctions between Reactive and failed[xli]. If we were artificial intelligence addicted futurologists, these factors would be a feature vector[340] rather than a single factor. Also, every recent world event of this type suggests build up and a final flashpoint[341].

---

340 In pattern recognition and machine learning, a feature vector is an n-dimensional vector of numerical features that represent some object.
341 Tarek el-Tayeb Mohamed Bouazizi was a Tunisian street vendor who set himself on fire on 17 December 2010, which became a catalyst for the Tunisian Revolution

The Algorithmic Anarchist   Hugh Barnard 24/10/21

The current, unexpected Gilet Jaune[xlii] protests in France have resulted in use of water cannon, ruined speed cameras, police excesses, deaths and blockaded roads. They have diminished somewhat because the French government has reversed a fuel tax rise. But food, water scarcity and price volatility caused by climate change *cannot be reversed in this way,* so one could expect a more persistent cycle of protest, panic and repression until the last few strands of state snap.

GLM Approach

I present three strands in this approach, material, technical and and societal. I believe that currently technocratic governments can mutate towards this path, assuming politicians of intelligence and humility. A great deal of the work, both material, technical and societal is, in fact an *undoing*, letting go of the big centre and strengthening the smaller local, towards physical preparation, mitigation and societal resilience.

The Material

First physical mitigation, steps towards both food and health can be taken via *deep greening the city*. Trees provide shade, are carbon sinks and fruit or nut trees provide food. Bushes provide more fruit. Thousands of pieces of grass, mown and remown for no apparent reason can provide space for variegated planting. Given the extremes of rainfall and temperature and constraints of space, the best model for this is a heat adapted version of the Forest Garden[xliii].

This is high density, low maintenance arrangement of productive plants, bushes and trees. In Nepal '*Home gardens, with their intensive and multiple uses, provide a safety net for households when food is scarce.*' So this activity is not necessarily a primary or sole source of food, for example, it is a safety net and also provides a counterbalance against price spikes. See the commentary on security and crime, later, to see how this produce is (not) protected.

The Algorithmic Anarchist   Hugh Barnard 24/10/21

Apart from the obvious areas to be re-purposed, there are, of course many private paved or tarmac areas used for parking or simply to avoid gardening in a time-poor, artificially stressed[xliv], urban society. There is already an American non-profit Depave.org[xlv] that reverses this.

Why is this a partial answer for health, also? Quite simply, tarmac is a black body that absorbs heat. Paving, concrete, and bricks (that we put in storage heaters, a clue) also act as heat storage. Vehicles, heating and air conditioning all output surplus heat. So, any city environment could benefit from tree-provided shade and re-greening at ground level, to mitigate high temperature and hence heat related health problems. Certain plants (ivy, for example) are also good pollution sinks, hedges help us and help wildlife too. There is some solid science in this paper[xlvi], part of the EPA collection, the EPA that the current US presidency is steadily dismantling.

Another part of the answer for health is cheap, available, and local fruit and vegetables, a problem for many modern urban diets, in spite of constant government propaganda. So we need to revive market gardening at the edge of the city. There are traces in Paris, at Maraichers[xlvii] (translation 'market gardens') in the 20th Arrondissement where, and, I quote *'Until the 20th century the hills of Belleville and Montreuil were cultivated by many market-gardeners, whose most famous products were the "peaches of Montreuil"'*. Outside London, patchwork and free gardens are already appearing[xlviii], too. This is a carbon footprint, food miles and pollution issue, it is logical to produce *some* food *near* consumption and return somewhat to the pleasant aspects of cyclic time (pace Debord) delineated by seasonal produce.

To summarise this physical character of the mitigated city, it is a maximal *rus in urbe,* an augmented version of Cleveland's Forest City[xlix]. A cool green, blue, and brown place filled with teeming life, solar panels, rain water harvesters, anaerobic composters and nearly emptied of motor transport, that a contemporary commentator called 'treescape'.

The Technical

Within the technical there are two strands, open knowledge[342] and alternative technology[343]. For the first, open knowledge (I include the world of open source software[344] and hardware), let us conduct a little thought experiment. So, the Acme corporation a for-profit has developed technology that will reverse global warming in two years. However, it is only prepared to sell it rather than gift it. Only rich countries can afford it and the solution needs world-wide application. So, everyone suffers and dies, *killed by intellectual property law, profit motive, and shareholder value.* Actually, in this case, I believe governments would become coercive, so this is a weak scenario.

---

342 Open knowledge is knowledge that one is free to use, reuse, and redistribute without legal, social or technological restriction.
343 Alternative technology refers to technologies that are more environmentally friendly than the functionally equivalent technologies dominant in current practice.
344 The open-source model is a decentralized software development model that encourages open collaboration. A main principle of open-source software development is peer production, with products such as source code, blueprints, and documentation freely available to the public.

The Algorithmic Anarchist   Hugh Barnard 24/10/21

But knowledge is not rivalrous, when I know something, you do not stop knowing it, for example. So, there are strong arguments, especially down at the two primary Maslow layers, for a culture of open, generous knowledge and (see the next section) open social epistemology to address our most pressing problems.

Some of the more obvious avenues, research projects in higher education and charities, for example, have been damaged, fragmented, privatised or compromised by grants, grant 'competition' and strings-attached funding and 'sponsorship' from commercial organisations already in the Standard Technocratic Model.

Next, and feeding into this, alternative technology. We can choose here, low power, passive technologies using alternative techniques and materials. For example, dry stone walls (fun to build too) are alternatives to concrete barriers and we should look to the tropics for new passive dwelling construction[1]. All these initiatives reduce the power expended, until there is steady convergence with levels of power that renewables produce.

We will still need steel and concrete, but we will need *less*. This passive, re-humanising trend will also carry into technology too, sensors rather than actuators[345], to report on the 'world' but leave us human agency and physicality to act. Why do people garden? Here is a clue that non-alienated, physical work in the air may be pleasurable.

---

345 An actuator is a component of a machine that is responsible for moving and controlling a mechanism or system. In simple terms, it is a "mover" rather than a "listener".

The Algorithmic Anarchist   Hugh Barnard 24/10/21

I doubt that the dream of full, luxury automation, even as full automated luxury communism[li] is desirable from many standpoints, from the physical health benefits to some more general notion of flourishing. Another complete essay with the epigraph 'Glory heere, Diggers all'[lii]!

The Social

Next, the social thread. As a concept that requires a complete essay (a book[liii], in fact) but needs a more compact discussion here, I advance the idea of *antisocial and social space*.

Antisocial, the architectural conveyor belt spaces for 'commercial browsing' without social connection. Fast food chains now have touch screens, customers order quickly without talking to the counter staff who can, of course, then be reduced in number. Obviously, cars isolate too, though as city folk we talk less than we *should*, even in shared public transport, for we are entranced by the contents of our electronic devices.

Our neighbourhood cafés close, replaced by expensive (and therefore exclusive) coffee chains where digital nomads sit silently peering into screens. Much of the apparent public realm is also now private and enclosed[liv], so no-one may sit, talk, sing or protest.

The Algorithmic Anarchist   Hugh Barnard 24/10/21

Finally, we close or convert our libraries or community centres, after all, there is 'austerity' and these items do not self-finance and the *numbers do not add up*. We close social space containing social activity and replace it by anti-social space supporting colonised (see Lefebvre[lv]) and transaction based activity.

Even our electronic communications, previously a neutral affair, remember the *telephone call*, are mediated by predatory vectorialists[346] and our meta-data (where are you, how many times have you contacted this person, from what phone model) is sucked out, commodified and sold, it may be *good to talk*, but the question lingers *for whom*? Neither the technocratic approach nor the reactive approach do any remedial work here, because anti-social space is a feature of a neo-liberal, technocratic narrative, money must change hands, even within the smallest human activity, comprehensively ignoring Sandel[lvi].

So, one important component of resilience in cities is the reclamation and re-creation of *social space*. These are neutral spaces that allow *people to meet* and activities to take place, things (yes, I am avoiding any rigid ontology) to happen. Unlike the grant driven, agenda focused, time limited (since the *numbers will not add up*, after a while) *leisure activities* that our governments are so terribly keen on. You may well ask, dear reader, what this has to do with ecology, mitigation and resilience? And, quite brazenly, I answer, *nothing directly*.

---

346 Wark, McKenzie. A Hacker Manifesto. Harvard University Press, 2004, p. 57
Wark calls the information producers "hackers," and refers to the owners/expropriators of information as "the vectorialist class" (since "information" travels along "vectors" as it is reproduced and transmitted).

However, *indirectly*, a different and more positive view emerges. That is, these are spaces for low level initiatives and problem solving, of which, resilience and mitigation activities are a subset.

They serve allotment users, guerilla gardeners, citizen scientists to meet, exchange and be convivial toolmakers[lvii]. At a meta level, there is value in physical meeting itself[lviii], as opposed to electronically mediated meetings. Physical sociability gives mental health benefits as an important collateral benefit. Also, logically, if climate problems inflict damage on the electronic infrastructure (for example, loss of telephone masts), our physical exchanges then also become a central part of our social resilience.

Two final benefits of social spaces, prevention of othering and social epistemology. When we meet, talk and undertake projects together we inoculate ourselves, against the othering that has reappeared as the xenophobic thread in our national life and the darker side of identity politics. We also improve trust by creating informal, non-cryptographic webs of trust[347], restoring that which has been destroyed by fake-name, anonymous and false-flag trolling in the attention economy of commercial cyberspace. If we are to be *all in it together*, we need to be *more together*.

---

347 Nicholas Pornin. (2018). What is Web of Trust?. Available: https://security.stackexchange.com/questions/61360/what-is-the-web-of-trust. Last accessed 15th January 2019.

The Algorithmic Anarchist	Hugh Barnard 24/10/21

Social space is a space for social epistemology too, problems get discussed and solved or set aside, for the moment, and marked as *Aporia*. Objectors may want this activity to take place exclusively online, but this disenfranchises the old, digitally challenged, second language speakers, the poor, and ethics-motivated cyber refuseniks.

The scope of 'grass roots' social epistemology is expanding too, from the philosophical towards citizen science, open knowledge and open source technology, as described earlier. There is a meta-benefit here too, de-transactionalised relations of generosity, it is pleasant to *eat, share and discover together*. For example, here is an open source tool for estimating tree cover[348], that my imagined municipality would find useful.

Last, social spaces permit the inception and reinforcement of an authentic pluralistic narrative and meta-narratives[349], as opposed to the ambient monolithic narrative of the Spectacle[lix] (or of Fascism, for example, coherent but not pluralistic) that haunts and occupies the totality of anti-social space, advertising, status, transaction, ambient alienation and pervasive verbal and non-verbal micro aggression, I'm so sorry I bumped into you, I was playing Candy Crush Saga. People really need to watch where they are going, don't they? Especially those weird people wandering around without phones, those are the worst, they are traitors to the Spectacle, since they are *not continually consuming*.

---

348 Various. (N.D.). OpenTreeMap. Available: http://opentreemap.github.io/. Last accessed 15th January 2019.
349 Wikipedia contributors. (2018, December 1). Twelve leverage points. In Wikipedia, The Free Encyclopedia. Retrieved 11:01, February 22, 2019, from https://en.wikipedia.org/w/index.php?title=Twelve_leverage_points&oldid=871537650

How about security and crime[350]? Again, this is another, complete essay. However, as with health and food supply, the effort is towards prevention, rather than sanction. This municipal microcosm has a non consumer, non competition narrative that values cooperation and generosity, rather than artificial scarcity and competition, partially a restatement of Kropotkin[351] *'Sociability is as much a law of nature as mutual struggle'*.

Some lessons have been absorbed from the Bourgeois Bohême too, contempt for consumer fetish, so the environment is not full of shiny things to steal. Local mutual social credit (see, for example, Lietaer[lx]) is used for local transactions, making financial theft rather more difficult and pointless. Drugs are legal but alcohol is discouraged and, a great deal of the alienation that is motivation for heavy drug use is removed. It is difficult to 'steal' from the public spaces, since *this is not stealing now*, see the Todmorden project[352] and offshoots.

---

350 Dr. Liz Levy, Dr Dharshi Santhakumaran, Dr Richard Whitecross. (2014). What Works to Reduce Crime?: A Summary of the Evidence. Available: https://www2.gov.scot/Resource/0046/00460517.pdf. Last accessed 15th January 2019.
351 Mutual Aid a Factor of Evolution/Chapter I. (2012, April 17). In Wikisource . Retrieved 10:15, February 1, 2019, from https://en.wikisource.org/w/index.php?title=Mutual_Aid_a_Factor_of_Evolution/Chapter_I&oldid=3802484
352 Wikipedia contributors. (2019, January 22). Incredible Edible. In Wikipedia, The Free Encyclopedia. Retrieved 11:59, February 5, 2019, from https://en.wikipedia.org/w/index.php?title=Incredible_Edible&oldid=879556925

Social space and activity, described above, displace much small scale criminal activity, petty theft, and vandalism resulting from boredom and a lack of alternatives. Apparently life chances are possibly improved too[353]. As in Vietnam, before Coca-Cola and other Western 'gifts', illiteracy is nearly unknown. There is not a direct causal connection between illiteracy and crime, but there is a high degree of correlation. Of course, I have not dealt with psychopathy (rather than sociopathy, which seems to stem from childhood abuse, something that can be addressed) and crimes of passion, here.

Concerning distributive justice towards harvest and prevention of misuse of the commons, a number of lessons have been taken from Ostrom's Eight Principles[354] for protecting and managing a common resource. For example, *5. Develop a system, carried out by community members, for monitoring members' behaviour* is via the mutual social credit system which is transparent for transactions concerning food and water. However, it is not transparent for other transactions, otherwise it would quickly take on the characteristics of the current Chinese social credit system[lxi].

---

353 Mahoney, Joseph L. "School Extracurricular Activity Participation as a Moderator in the Development of Antisocial Patterns." Child Development, vol. 71, no. 2, 2000, pp. 502–516. JSTOR, www.jstor.org/stable/1132005.
354 Jay Walljasper. (2011). Elinor Ostrom's 8 Principles for Managing a Commons.Available: http://www.onthecommons.org/magazine/elinor-ostroms-8-principles-managing-commmons. Last accessed 15th January 2019.

Conclusions

I am very pessimistic about the first two approaches, the technocratic and reactive, because, apart from the specific arguments in the body of the essay, I believe that the many modern Western governments suffer from *infrastructural failure*, vested interests, politicians with second jobs, without life experience, with drug, alcohol or mental health problems, special advisors without life experience, weak donation and contribution rules, game playing instead of leadership, weak oversight and governance structures, first past post elections, non-rotation of elected officials, hidden lobbying (and in the USA, actual drafting of laws[355]), non-transparent funding of 'think tanks', monolithic approaches to the 'economy', the forgotten or derided concept of a 'political economy'.

So I hope to have shown why adopting GLM provides a useful, coherent, pragmatic and attractive path and narrative at municipal level. Also, why the two alternatives, I have described contain one partial dead end, the Standard Technocratic and one related unattractive, violent path, the Reactive.

---

355 Alisa Chang. (2013). When Lobbyists Literally Write the Bill. Available: https://www.npr.org/sections/itsallpolitics/2013/11/11/243973620/when-lobbyists-literally-write-the-bill. Last accessed 15th January 2019.

The Algorithmic Anarchist   Hugh Barnard 24/10/21

My positive arguments concentrate on the local, the municipal, where, we have some direct official and plenty of unofficial agency. They do not create agency or renewal at a national level, but may help to create a new narrative that *prefigures* national changes of policy, national governments are increasingly *followers* now that the public have social media groups that sometimes morph into effective praxis[lxii].

My borough, the basis for this thought experiment, is experimenting with citizen's assemblies and participatory budgeting[356], following some of Bookchin's municipal ideas. The relationship between the municipal and the national may remain uneasy, with bolder municipality and atrophy/fragmentation of the Standard Technocratic centre.

With any increase in local or municipal *actual* resource self sufficiency, the lever and threat of central government money, traditionally used from the centre downwards has a more limited effect. The creation and 'liberation' of public space is not 'expensive' either legally or financially and open knowledge is, well, usually free, always open.

---

356 Wikipedia contributors. (2019, January 10). Participatory budgeting. In Wikipedia, The Free Encyclopedia. Retrieved 07:22, January 21, 2019, from https://en.wikipedia.org/w/index.php?title=Participatory_budgeting&oldid=877719329

But municipal level action does not mitigate or solve some of the larger inputs to atmospheric pollution. The top hundred sources produce 71% of emissions[357], and therefore, they *are* beyond the grasp of local mitigation. However, for the most part, we are still wage-slaves and our kindly owners provide pension funds that *do* currently invest in fossil extractive companies.

The more enlightened organisations and universities have already started to divest. About 5% of global carbon dioxide release is associated with concrete manufacture[358], so arguably, my imagined municipality should use some wooden structures as in times past. Even though we must 'forget' British colonialists 'So little done, so much to do' - Cecil Rhodes.

---

[357] Wikipedia contributors. (2018, August 25). Top contributors to carbon dioxide emissions. In Wikipedia, The Free Encyclopedia. Retrieved 07:13, January 21, 2019, from https://en.wikipedia.org/w/index.php?title=Top_contributors_to_carbon_dioxide_emissions&o

[358] Wikipedia contributors. (2019, January 13). Environmental impact of concrete. In Wikipedia, The Free Encyclopedia. Retrieved 10:28, January 16, 2019, from https://en.wikipedia.org/w/index.php?title=Environmental_impact_of_concrete&oldid=878101233

The Algorithmic Anarchist   Hugh Barnard 24/10/21

No single grand ethical or political theory or technology can address climate change either, so I remain steadfast within ethical and political contextual approaches. Two final quotes, about the non-normative, meta-journey:

"My focus on infrastructures will be an attempt to diversify and pluralise this discussion, partly by pointing to the multiplicity of underpinnings that need to be put in place for achieving sustainability on any scale—not simply science and technology, but also economics, ethics, law, and politics. I want to advocate for more experimental but also more participatory approaches to future-making, not propelled mainly by what is (or is thought to be) technologically feasible, but more fundamentally by diverse human imaginations of what might be good and attainable worlds."
- Prof Sheila Jasanoff[lxiii] Harvard Kennedy School

"Much that is terrible we do not know. Much that is beautiful we shall still discover. Let's sail till we come to the edge." - Thomas M. Disch at the end of Camp Concentration[lxiv]

Bibliography

i   Raymond Geuss (2008). Philosophy and Real Politics. Cambridge: Princeton University Press. 1-10.
ii Levitas R. (2013). Utopia as Method. UK: Pallgrave Macmillan. 1-220.
iii Murray Bookchin (1990). Remaking Society. Boston: South End Press. 1-114 (available at https://libcom.org/files/RemakingSociety.pdf)
iv Herman Kahn & Anthony J. Wiener. (N.D.). The Use of Scenarios. Available: https://www.hudson.org/research/2214-the-use-of-scenarios. Last accessed 7 May 2019.
v   Various. (2019). Net Zero – The UK's contribution to stopping global warming.Available: https://www.theccc.org.uk/publication/net-zero-the-uks-contribution-to-stopping-global-warming/. Last accessed 2 May 2019.
vi David Lewis (1986). The Plurality of Worlds. USA: Wiley-Blackwell. 288.
vii Gerla, G.; Transformational semantics for first order logic, Logique et Analyse, No. 117–118, pp. 69–79, 1987.
viii Øhrstrøm, Peter and Hasle, Per, "Future Contingents", The Stanford Encyclopedia of Philosophy (Winter 2015 Edition), Edward N. Zalta (ed.), URL = <https://plato.stanford.edu/archives/win2015/entries/future-contingents/>.
ix Smiley, Marion, "Collective Responsibility", The Stanford Encyclopedia of Philosophy (Summer 2017 Edition), Edward N. Zalta (ed.), URL = <https://plato.stanford.edu/archives/sum2017/entries/collective-responsibility/>.
x   Raymond Geuss (2008). Philosophy and Real Politics. Cambridge: Princeton University Press. 1-10.
xi Ruppel, C. D. (2011) Methane Hydrates and Contemporary Climate Change. Nature Education Knowledge 3(10):29
xii Wikipedia contributors. (N.D.). Stratospheric Aerosol Injection. Available: https://en.wikipedia.org/wiki/Stratospheric_aerosol_injection. Last accessed 29th October 2018.
xiii Mark Lynas (2007). Six Degrees. London: Fourth Estate. 1-360.
xiv DEFRA. (2018). Food Statistics in Your Pocket. Available: https://www.gov.uk/government/publications/food-statistics-pocketbook-2017/food-statistics-in-your-pocket-2017-global-and-uk-supply. Last accessed 29th October 2018.
xv DEFRA. (2018). Food Statistics in Your Pocket. Available: https://www.gov.uk/government/publications/food-statistics-

pocketbook/food-statistics-in-your-pocket-prices-and-expenditure. Last accessed 29th October 2018.
xvi Various. (N.D.). Can the UK feed itself after Brexit. Available: https://www.countryfile.com/news/can-the-uk-feed-itself-after-brexit/. Last accessed 15th January 2019.
xvii Morison, J. I. L. and Matthews, R. B. (eds.) (2016): Agriculture and Forestry Climate Change Impacts Summary Report, Living With Environmental Change. ISBN 978-0-9934074-0-6 copyright © Living With Environmental Change.
xviii Various. (2017). UK Climate Risk Assessment 2017. Available: https://assets.publishing.service.gov.uk/government/uploads/system/uploads/attachment_data/file/584281/uk-climate-change-risk-assess-2017.pdf. Last accessed 29th October 2018.
xix Martin Armstrong. (2017). How Thirsty is Our Food?. Available: https://www.statista.com/chart/9483/how-thirsty-is-our-food/. Last accessed 15th January 2019.
xx Sarah Knapton. (2014). World War 2 left toxic legacy of ill health and depression.Available: https://www.telegraph.co.uk/history/world-war-two/10584595/World-War-2-left-toxic-legacy-of-ill-health-and-depression.html. Last accessed 29th October 2018
xxi Wikipedia contributors. (N.D.). 2003 European heat wave. Available: https://en.wikipedia.org/wiki/2003_European_heat_wave. Last accessed 29th October 2018.
xxii Wikipedia contributors. (N.D.). Wicked Problem. Available: https://en.wikipedia.org/wiki/Wicked_problem. Last accessed 29th October 2018.
xxiii Various. (2019). Net Zero – The UK's contribution to stopping global warming.Available: https://www.theccc.org.uk/publication/net-zero-the-uks-contribution-to-stopping-global-warming/. Last accessed 2 May 2019.
xxiv Broome, John (1994). Discounting the Future. _Philosophy and Public Affairs_ 23 (2):128-156. and Counting the Cost of Global Warming.
xxv Fabio RubioScarano. (2017). Ecosystem-based adaptation to climate change: concept, scalability and a role for conservation science. Perspectives in Ecology and Conservation. 15 (2), 65-73.
xxvi Various. (2019). Net Zero – The UK's contribution to stopping global warming.Available: https://www.theccc.org.uk/publication/net-zero-the-uks-contribution-to-stopping-global-warming/. Last accessed 4 May 2019.
xxvii Teresa Zolch, Christine Wamsler, Stephan Pauleit, Integrating the ecosystem-based approach into municipal climate adaptation strategies:

The case of Germany Teresa. Journal of Cleaner Production 170 (2018) 966 – 977

xxviii Wikipedia contributors. (2019, January 12). WHO Model List of Essential Medicines. In Wikipedia, The Free Encyclopedia. Retrieved 16:07, January 19, 2019, from https://en.wikipedia.org/w/index.php?title=WHO_Model_List_of_Essential_Medicines&oldid=87801446

xxix Wikipedia contributors. (N.D.). Food Riots. Available: https://en.wikipedia.org/wiki/List_of_food_riots. Last accessed 29th October 2018

xxx Wikipedia contributors. (2018, November 24). Fuel protests in the United Kingdom. In Wikipedia, The Free Encyclopedia. Retrieved 11:29, January 31, 2019, from https://en.wikipedia.org/w/index.php?title=Fuel_protests_in_the_United_Kingdom&oldid=870365987

xxxi John O'Neill. (2017). Life Beyond Capital. Available: https://www.cusp.ac.uk/themes/m/m1-6/. Last accessed 29th October 2018.

xxxii Richard Grant. (2018). Do Trees Talk to Each Other?. Available: https://www.smithsonianmag.com/science-nature/the-whispering-trees-180968084/. Last accessed 29th October 2018.

xxxiii Edmund Burke. (N.D.). Danger of Abstract Views. Available: http://gutenberg.readingroo.ms/3/2/8/3286/3286-h/3286-h.htm. Last accessed 15th January 2019.

xxxiv Debord, Guy, 1970, *The Society of the Spectacle*, Detroit: Black and Red.

xxxv Bill Murphy. (N.D.). Forget Free Hugs. Available: https://www.inc.com/bill-murphy-jr/forget-free-hugs-now-you-can-make-80-to-100-an-hour-as-a-professional-cuddler.html. Last accessed 29th October 2018.

xxxvi Various. (11 October 2017). Atlas Network. Available: https://www.sourcewatch.org/index.php/Atlas_Network. Last accessed 29th October 2018.

xxxvii Fried, B. (1995). Wilt Chamberlain Revisited: Nozick's "Justice in Transfer" and the Problem of Market-Based Distribution. Philosophy & Public Affairs, 24(3), 226-245.

xxxviii Naomi Klein (2007). The Shock Doctrine: The Rise of Disaster Capitalism. London: Allen Lane. 1-576.

xxxix WOLFF, R. P. (1970). In defense of anarchism. New York, Harper & Row.

xl Various. (2018). Fragile States Index. Available: http://fundforpeace.org/fsi/country-data/. Last accessed 29th October 2018.

xli Wikipedia contributors. (N.D.). Creeping Normality. Available: https://en.wikipedia.org/wiki/Creeping_normality. Last accessed 29th October 2018.

xlii Wikipedia contributors. (2019, May 14). Yellow vests movement. In Wikipedia, The Free Encyclopedia. Retrieved 10:38, May 14, 2019, from https://en.wikipedia.org/w/index.php?title=Yellow_vests_movement&oldid=896977688

xliii Various. (N.D.). The Forest Garden. Available: https://www.permaculture.org.uk/practical-solutions/forest-gardens. Last accessed 7 May 2019.

xliv David Graeber (2018). Bullshit Jobs. New York: Simon & Schuster. 1-300.

xlv Various. (N.D.). Depave. Available: https://depave.org/. Last accessed 29th October 2018.

xlvi H. Akbari, M. Pomerantz and H. Taha. (2001). Cool Surfaces And Shade Trees To Reduce Energy Use And Improve Air Quality In Urban Areas. Solar Energy. 70 (3), 3, pp. 295–310.

xlvii Wikipedia contributors. (N.D.). Maraichers (Metro). Available: https://en.wikipedia.org/wiki/Mara%C3%AEchers_(Paris_M%C3%A9tro). Last accessed 29th October 2018.

xlviii Wikipedia contributors. (N.D.). Incredible Edible. Available: https://en.wikipedia.org/wiki/Incredible_Edible. Last accessed 29th October 2018.

xlix Various. (2019). Forest City. Available: https://case.edu/ech/articles/f/forest-city. Last accessed 12th January 2019.

l Adinda Septi Hendriani, Hermawan and Banar Retyanto. (2017). Comparison analysis of wooden house thermal comfort in tropical coast and mountainous by using wall surface temperature difference. Available: https://aip.scitation.org/doi/abs/10.1063/1.5003490

li Aaron Bastani (2019). Full Automated Luxury Communism. London: Verso. 288.

lii Various. (N.D.). Levellers and Diggers. Available: http://www.diggers.org/diggers/digg_eb.html. Last accessed 15th January 2019.

liii Eric Klinenberg (2018). Palaces for the People. London: Penguin Random House.

liv Anna Minton (2012). Ground Control. London: Penguin. 1-228.

lv Critique de la vie quotidienne, III: De la modernité au modernisme

(pour une metaphilosophie du quotidien), Paris: L'Arche, 1981.
lvi Sandel Michael J. 2012. What Money Can't Buy: The Moral Limits of Markets. Farrar, Straus and Giroux.
lvii Ivan Illich. (1973). Tools for Conviviality. Available: https://comunity.net/system/files/ILLICH%201973_tools_for_convivality_1.pdf. Last accessed 15th January 2019.
lviii Susan Pinker (2015). The Village Effect : Why Face-to-face Contact Matters. London: Atlantic Books. 1-432.
lix Debord, Guy, 1970, *The Society of the Spectacle*, Detroit: Black and Red.
lx Lietaer, Bernard. The Future of Money. Random House, 2001.
lxi Wikipedia contributors. (2019, May 11). Social Credit System. In Wikipedia, The Free Encyclopedia. Retrieved 09:08, May 13, 2019, from https://en.wikipedia.org/w/index.php?title=Social_Credit_System&oldid=896612827
lxii Wikipedia contributors. (2019, May 6). Extinction Rebellion. In Wikipedia, The Free Encyclopedia. Retrieved 18:03, May 6, 2019, from https://en.wikipedia.org/w/index.php?title=Extinction_Rebellion&oldid=895814729
lxiii Various. (N.D.). Sheila Jasanoff. Available: https://www.hks.harvard.edu/faculty/sheila-jasanoff. Last accessed 15th January 2019.
lxiv Wikipedia contributors. (2018, May 30). Camp Concentration. In Wikipedia, The Free Encyclopedia. Retrieved 17:25, January 21, 2019, from https://en.wikipedia.org/w/index.php?title=Camp_Concentration&oldid=843636006

L - #0123 - 101121 - C0 - 210/148/9 - PB - DID3194316